NO

I KNOW IT WHEN I SEE IT

I KNOW IT WHEN I SEE IT

Pornography, Violence, and Public Sensitivity

by
Michael Leach

THE WESTMINSTER PRESS
Philadelphia

Book Design by Dorothy Alden Smith

Published by The Westminster Press®
Philadelphia, Pennsylvania

PRINTED IN THE UNITED STATES OF AMERICA

Library of Congress Cataloging in Publication Data

Leach, Michael, 1940–
    I know it when I see it.

    Bibliography: p.
    1. Sex in moving-pictures.   2. Violence in moving-
pictures.   I. Title.
PN1995.9.S45L4   791.43′0909′353   75–23017
ISBN 0–664–20800–2

For my mother and father,
who took me to a cowboy movie
called *The Outlaw*
when I was six years old

I suspect that I am, far more than not, in your own situation: deeply interested in moving pictures, considerably experienced from childhood on in watching them and thinking and talking about them, and totally, or almost totally, without experience or even much second-hand knowledge of how they are made. If I am broadly right in this assumption, we start on the same ground, and under the same handicaps, and I qualify to be here, if at all, only by two means. It is my business to conduct one end of a conversation, as an amateur critic among amateur critics. And I will be of use and interest only in so far as my amateur judgment is sound, stimulating, or illuminating.

—JAMES AGEE, 1942

CONTENTS

PREVIEW

"38,000 couples have seen this show," boasts the ad in *The New York Times*. "The Rolls Royce of Hardcore," it rolls on. "Sex as ritual, sex as fantasy, sex as it could be only in the movies . . . A MARILYN CHAMBERS Double Feature . . . *Behind the Green Door* and *Resurrection of Eve*." As of this morning, Marilyn Chambers is an American cultural phenomenon. She has a dual claim to fame: her angelic face shines on millions of Ivory Snow boxes in homes across the land while the rest of her writhes on feverish films that show to curious couples as well as to the mythical man with a raincoat on his lap. That 38,000 figure is a New York statistic, but couples watch Marilyn in other cities too—except where the police have confiscated the reels.

Farther down the page of the same *Times,* stone-faced Charles Bronson, another cultural phenomenon, points a handgun in the direction of your face. "A Time-Bomb of a Movie," runs the blurb. "So timely in its terror that the switchblade seems to prick the viewer's skin, the bullet seems to whiz along his ear. . . . When Charles Bronson begins to shoot the bad guys, it's difficult not to cheer him on with loud shouts of encouragement." *Death Wish* is the smash of the season, outgrossing (in several ways) *The Godfather* in many theaters from coast to coast. The message of the movie, says critic Vincent Canby, is simple: "Kill. Try it. You'll like it." The film has never been confiscated by local police and will probably appear on your television screen sometime during the bicentennial.

At the bottom of the page, a modest ad informs you: "The United States Supreme Court has ruled that *Carnal Knowledge* is *not obscene*. See it now!" You may recall that this popular Mike Nichols movie, with a screenplay by Jules Feiffer, was critically acclaimed in 1971 as a heavy commentary on the emptiness of aggressive, self-seeking sex. In 1973, however, the Supreme Court ruled that books or films with sexual themes not only must have "redeeming social value" but must have specific "literary, artistic, political or scientific" value as well and that local, not national, standards are the criteria for judging if a given work meets this test. Sure enough, it wasn't long until citizens of Albany, Georgia, convicted Billy Jenkins, a theater manager, for showing *Carnal Knowledge*.

The case was appealed in 1974 and, as the ad indicates, Billy Jenkins got to stay home. The theme of the movie was entirely sexual, and certain scenes fairly sizzled, especially a nude shot of Ann-Margret that particularly angered the Albanians. Justice William Rehnquist was careful to point out, however, that the camera did not focus on Jack Nicholson's "genitals, lewd or otherwise, during these scenes," and therefore *Carnal Knowledge* was not legally obscene. Yes, it is a rather male chauvinistic statement, but, more significantly, it further obfuscates what is or is not pornography under the new standards. At about the same time, citizens of Drake, North Dakota, used these standards to burn thirty-two copies of Kurt Vonnegut's *Slaughter-House Five*.

What makes a movie obscene? What is pornography? Do *Carnal Knowledge* and *Behind the Green Door* belong in the same category? Or is *Green Door* closer in spirit to *Death Wish?* And which of these is more obscene? Should we wish to censor either of them?

I don't want to get lost in the legal labyrinth of pornography, but I do wish to explore some of the principles behind the blue door. Educator Richard Hettlinger points out one of them: "The implication is that sex is so virulent a danger that it requires special restriction lest it threaten the whole fabric of society. Almost any scene of violence or sadistic torture is assumed to be without serious deleterious effect on the young; but the sight of a female breast or of the human genitals is assumed to be immediately depraving."

A Los Angeles *Times* film critic illustrates the paradox. He went to see *The Moment of Truth,* a semidocumentary about a bullfighter, and found a seat behind a mother and her little boy. As scene after scene of stabbing and bleeding splashed across the screen, the reviewer, revulsed, "turned away again and again," while the mother and child, sharing a box of popcorn, sat transfixed. But when a candid love scene flashed on the screen, "the mother reached over and placed a hand across her son's eyes."

I'd like to discuss the paradox of pornography in the context of movies, too. The truth is concrete, and movies, more than any other medium, mirror the ways we think and feel. The movies that I'll be discussing are mostly those I either sneaked in to see as a kid, paid my way in as an adult, or have seen on television from the age of ten until today. You'll be familiar with many of them too.

Until recently, the only hard-core sex film I had seen was the socially acceptable (at least within the decadent, Eastern circle I move in) *Deep Throat.* While I thought that movie was certainly immature if not grossly immodest, I also had to admit that the legerdemain of its star, the legendary Linda Lovelace, surely had at least "scientific value," and that the movie's intent was not nearly as immoral as *Super Fly,* one that lionizes a dope peddler and was playing to a packed house of cheering teen-agers when I had seen it the previous week.

I decided to do some research through books and looks and put together a perspective on pornography that would combine a gentle sense of humor with a little common sense. As I'm sure you've guessed, my hope was not to narrow down the concept of obscenity in order to help eliminate pornography but to stretch it in order to increase awareness about ourselves.

I also confess that I found the prospect of doing some necessary research around Times Square darkly appealing. I could now satisfy my curiosity by seeing what the "Rolls Royce of Hardcore" was all about without being embarrassed if I saw my next-door neighbor walking in as I was going out. "I'm writing a book, Jack. What's your excuse?"

Before you and I go to the show together, I'd like to take this moment outside to thank my wonderful wife, Vickie—not only for her love and encouragement, but for cheerfully explaining to our children that Daddy still loved them while he played with his typewriter in the basement below. If more of us were like her, there'd be little need for any pornography at all.

M.L.

Old Greenwich
Winter 1975

REEL ONE

A Definition of Pornography

"As a father and a grandfather, I know, by golly, what is obscene and what isn't."

—SENATOR BARRY GOLDWATER

[The 1970 American Commission on Obscenity was shocked to discover that "none of the federal statutes prohibiting 'obscene' materials defines that term."]

"I don't believe that the word 'obscene' can *ever* be properly, conclusively defined," says psychologist Albert Ellis.

Actually, anyone can define obscenity. Obscene is disgusting, loathsome, repulsive, revolting, indecent, ugly, offensive to the senses, or, in the words of my four-year-old son, "just plain yucchy." In legal terms, obscenity tends to "corrupt or deprave." The word has recently come to be associated with pornography, which, in addition to all of the above, has something to do with sex.

And that's where confusion sets in.

The only definition of pornography that everyone seems to agree on is the one given by Justice Stewart Potter in 1964: "I know it when I see it." Pornography, in other words, exists in the mind of the beholder, but if it can be defined only subjectively, one has to wonder if it can exist objectively.

Henry Miller, who should know something about it, says

that talking about "the nature and meaning of pornography is almost as difficult as talking about God." D. H. Lawrence, who also had a stake in the issue, wryly remarks, "What is pornography to one man is the laughter of genius to another." Historian Richard Randall, an innocent observer, calls it "the most familiar and the most elusive of concepts in law and social life."

"Pornography must be important," says librarian Ervin Gaines, "or it would not be so prevalent. It has some meaning in our lives that we do not understand."

It is generally agreed that the word "pornography" applies to certain pictures, publications, or films that show nudity or sexual activity in a way that violates contemporary standards of propriety. But no judge or lawyer, priest or artist, critic or cop, has yet found a way to literally flesh out those standards in terms acceptable to society at large. Experts agree that the purpose of pornography is to excite people in some way, but they disagree on the effects of this stimulation. Some say it corrupts. Others say it is good for you. Still others insist it does neither, but "only thinking makes it so."

The word comes from the Greek words *pornē,* meaning "whore," and *graphein,* "to write": "to write a whore." The analogy goes something like this: in prostitution, one human uses another human as a sexual object, presumably debasing that person and humiliating oneself by having to pay for something one ought to be able to get for free. In pornography, a human being uses *an object* as an object, but again strictly for impersonal, nonthreatening sexual stimulation, and is presumably degraded by paying for a fantasy that society at large finds indecent.

What society at large finds indecent, or obscene, varies from culture to culture. The Soviet Union, for instance, has harsh restrictions against depictions of sex and violence. Denmark has no restrictions against sex but is harsh on violence. The United States seems to be in favor of violence but is down on sex.

The concept of what is obscene, or pornographic, also varies from era to era within any given culture. The obscenity of yesterday is not necessarily the pornography of today, and the pornography of today may pale in comparison to the obscenity of tomorrow. Jack Valenti, who once said he could go to bed at peace each night knowing Lyndon Johnson was President, had something milder to say as president of the Motion Picture Association of America: "What you and I believe to be obscene may not be so at all to the educated young. What they consider real and honest, you and I might view as coarse and ugly. Who is right? Each generation in its own turn shapes and forms the mores and the moral sense of the community. Change is endemic in every civilized community."

Existentially then, pornography might best be defined as a frontier phenomenon, encompassing specific material considered out-of-bounds by a specific culture at a specific time. As psychiatrist Irving Schneider points out, it is that one step beyond, simply by power of position, that stirs the senses and causes controversy.

In 1946, for instance, Howard Hughes's movie *The Outlaw* outraged half of America because Jane Russell exposed an extra inch of cleavage as she rolled in a haystack with Billy the Kid. When I was six years old, my parents took me with them to see that movie. It was just after the war and I imagine they couldn't afford a baby-sitter and probably figured I'd enjoy the cowboy stuff and fall asleep during the mushy parts. To this day, I remember vividly every detail from one particular scene: one in which Walter Huston shoots off Jack Buetel's ears, bit by bloody bit.

As Howard Hughes flew off into the sunset, *The Outlaw* was soon forgotten too—replaced in the public imagination

by a box-office smash called *Brute Force,* a prison melodrama in which Hume Cronyn as a Fascist guard rips Burt
Lancaster's face with a rubber hose while playing a record
of *Tannhäuser.* Ironically, no kid could get in to see *The
Outlaw* without his parents, but I do recall getting in to a
re-release of *Brute Force* with my pals when I was about ten.
It wasn't out-of-bounds.

Ten years after *The Outlaw,* in 1956, Elia Kazan's *Baby
Doll* was condemned by the Legion of Decency and de-
nounced in pulpits across the land; few, if any, clergy actually saw the movie or could say precisely why it was obscene;
it was obscene because Carol Baker, sucking her thumb, and
Eli Wallach, picking his nose, sweat a lot as they stared at
each other. Today "baby doll" is better known as a descrip-
tive term for a style of skimpy pajamas. But does anyone
remember why *The Moon Is Blue* caused such a storm? It
was recently shown on television, but few people bothered to
watch, missing the use of the word "virgin." In the '50s that
was out-of-bounds.

Within bounds was *The Big Heat,* which appeared the
same year the moon turned blue and turned the big screen
red. A popular thriller, it features Lee Marvin as a thug who
burns Gloria Grahame's face with scalding coffee, blows up
Jocelyn Brando with TNT, but finally meets justice as Glenn
Ford beats his skull against a wall. We all got a kick out of
that flick.

A decade later, Sidney Lumet's *The Pawnbroker,* based on
an acclaimed novel by Edward Lewis Wallant that dealt with
the twin obscenities of genocide and poverty, had to fight for
a Motion Picture Seal because bare bosoms were flashed in
two brief scenes. Believe it or not, it was at about the same
time that the Board of Censors in both New York and
Chicago snipped the scene of a baby bison being born in a
Walt Disney wildlife movie, while remaining deaf to the roar

of a gang of movies that glorified motorcycle thugs. Hell's Angels ride on the edge of the American frontier while a baby buffalo is born out-of-bounds.

Curiously, no one ever complained in those days about a series of Doris Day movies in which the plot was not so different from many racy movies today. Remember how Doris would resist the advances of Rock Hudson or James Garner for three reels, and then in the fourth, through a male maneuver or plot twist, her inhibitions would slip away as fast as the bed sheets, just in time for THE END? You were never allowed to see Miss Day's freckled flesh, but you were exposed (at a Saturday matinee and with your parents' permission) to a viewpoint of sexual values that may be more mindless and myopic than anything you'll get from *The Devil in Miss Jones*. Miss Jones's sin was to take her *Pillow Talk* a step or two beyond.

More recently, Americans argued over *Last Tango in Paris*, a rather boring movie, but one, like *Carnal Knowledge*, that deals seriously with a sexual theme in such a way as to bring both cheers and jeers. The central question usually asked at a cocktail party is, "Why didn't Marlon Brando take *his* underwear off?" The central question the movie asks is also an ethical one: "Is it possible to engage in fun sex without damaging, personal consequences?" And the movie's answer is "no." To make the point more vividly, the director crosses the frontier and blesses a marriage between content and form, leading to accusations of licentiousness, even though the message of the film is a traditionally moral one.

On the one hand, when *Last Tango* danced away to join *Baby Doll* as a soiled partner in movie history, an action flick called *Three the Hard Way* crept into town, and few people uttered a word. Starring Jim Brown, Fred Williamson, and Jim Kelly, it begins with a band of white men who plot to poison a ghetto water supply so that all black children will die of a disease resembling sickle-cell anemia. The movie goes on to show how the three black superheroes uncover the plot and maim, stomp, and shoot down the villains in vivid hues of red, black, and blue. As I write this, the movie is enjoying a run at neighborhood theaters in New Jersey, Long Island, and Connecticut—apparently a family film. On the side of the avenging angel, an American tradition, the three superheroes have all six feet within bounds.

On the other hand, so did *Topsy and Eva* in 1927. Here is how the American Film Institute describes that specific "black" film that played to that specific culture in that specific time:

"Topsy is one of the most damning examples of racist portraiture in the American film: she is ignorant, thieving, superstitious, undisciplined, uneducated, and given over to swearing and biting; she eats bugs picked from flowers and butts heads with a goat. And she is repeatedly characterized as dirty. After she is sold at auction for five cents to Little Eva, Topsy is given her first bath; she fights against the water, and a dog, after sniffing in disgust at her old clothes, takes them out and buries them. The dirt, however, seems to be more symbolic than real, for dirt is somehow equated with being black ('I won't ask you to make me white as Eva—just a nice light tan will do'), and the color of her skin is understood to be the badness of her character. *Topsy and Eva* has the elements of a Christian parable: Topsy, the bad child, is bad because she is black; she becomes good by following the example of Little Eva, the good white child. The film is about a black character redeemed by becoming white in all things except color. And color is the one thing that will never wash away."

Topsy, in case you're curious, was acted by Vivian Duncan, a white actress who started in show business as a yodeler in burlesque.

Portrayals of blacks in movies seem to have moved from one frontier to another. From *Green Pastures* to *The Edge of the City* to *Top of the Heap*. From *The Song of the South* to *Sweet Sweetback's Baadasssss Song*. From Stepin Fetchit to Sidney Poitier to Super Fly. But if the white racism of *Topsy and Eva* seems more obscene than the black racism of *Three the Hard Way*, that doesn't make the latter any less obscene. Perhaps the worst obscenity is that the most brutal of exploitation movies, black and white, are made by colorless people simply out to make a buck without a care for consequences.

One thing is certain then, in movies as in life, and that is the inevitability of change. Homosexuals, for instance, are another minority generally treated in movies as they are pictured by the culture in the times the movies are made. In 1941's *The Maltese Falcon*, Sydney Greenstreet and Elisha Cook trade lurid looks at each other. In 1961's *Spartacus*, at least Kirk Douglas and Tony Curtis look nice, but they too are content to make moo-moo eyes at each other as Curtis gasps at his death, "I love ya, Spotakiss."

In 1965, however, Rock Hudson pretends to be a "fairy" in order to seduce *A Very Special Favor* from Leslie Caron, establishing a stereotype that would last for years. Comedians like Jerry Lewis would characterize homosexuals as pansies on television, and if you were a male teen-ager at the time, you may have done the same to prove you were straight. In 1968, a ghastly gay year, *The Detective* Frank Sinatra discovers to his disgust that most of Manhattan is inhabited by screaming "faggots," *The Sergeant* Rod Steiger learns that he is a "sickie" who can't tell his penis from his pistol, and Susannah York reveals herself as a "closet butch" responsible for *The Killing of Sister George*.

In between, there are serious but partial attempts at understanding. *The Children's Hour*, with Shirley MacLaine and

Audrey Hepburn, shows how bigotry can destroy already hurt human lives. *A View from the Bridge* gives us a view of a tortured man who lusts after his niece and, in a moment of crazed confusion, plants a kiss on his rival's lips. And Marlon Brando, in a bravura but embarrassing performance, explores the ambiguity of sexuality through *Reflections in a Golden Eye.*

It wasn't until the X-rated *Midnight Cowboy* in 1969, showing the simple intimacy of two men this side of homosexuality, that the path was paved for films like the Emmy-award-winning *That Certain Summer,* showing the complex intimacy of two men on the other side of homosexuality, as well as for realistic explorations like *The Boys in the Band* and graphic exploitations like *Twilight Cowboy* and *The Boys in the Sand.*

But which of all the above treatments of homosexuals in movies seem to you the most obscene? Movies like *Twilight Cowboy* or movies like *A Very Special Favor?*

What applies to persons or groups also applies to themes. Abortion was out-of-bounds in films until it became a red herring in the 1951 *Detective Story.* In 1956, Carol Lynley wearing *Blue Denim* can consider it as long as she doesn't have one. In 1964, Natalie Wood, through *Love with the Proper Stranger,* can have one as long as the audience sees how grisly it is. By 1969, with the rise of the feminist movement, abortion becomes not a red herring but the whole plot point of another mystery called *Daddy's Gone-a-Hunting,* which few people bothered to see. And now we all know about *Maude.*

Except, some people in some parts of the country were not allowed to see the two-part program because other people decided it was obscene and, by pressuring their local CBS affiliates, saw to it that nobody in the area could see it.

Now which of all the above do you find the most offensive or obscene?

Did you know that the mere mention of rape was out-of-bounds until Stephen McNally jumped over a fence to ravish Jane Wyman as *Johnny Belinda* in 1948? It soon became a key element in dozens of movies after, from American films like *Peyton Place* and *A Streetcar Named Desire* to foreign classics like *Rashomon* and *The Virgin Spring*. These serious movies, of course, also paved the way for vulgarities like *Waterhole Three*, in which debonair James Coburn fluffs it off as "assault with a deadly weapon," and Sam Peckinpah's *Straw Dogs*, which tries to show that rape means never having to say please. But the crudities also laid the groundwork for films like *Cry Rape*, one of the most widely viewed television movies in 1974 and one that helped to put bite into the new rape laws already a reality in many states.

What applies to persons or groups or themes also applies to words. It's hard to believe that when Wendy Hiller blurted out "not bloody likely" in the 1938 *Pygmalion*, the audience blushed. In the 1964 remake, *My Fair Lady*, director George Cukor had Audrey Hepburn shout instead, "Move your bloomin' arse," and the audience laughed. We can only imagine what Eliza Doolittle would say today.

Two years later, the language barrier began to self-destruct as Elizabeth Taylor and Richard Burton hurled epithets at each other in *Who's Afraid of Virginia Woolf?* "At least," thought the centurions of the moral frontier, "this damn movie doesn't have a chance in hell of making it to television." Two years before CBS decided that *Virginia Woolf* was nothing to be afraid of, words like "damn" and "hell" had lost their shock value on television as well as in films.

But do you know the name of the first American star to use that most forbidden of all four-letter words in a film?

Oddly enough, it was again that former ingenue of *National Velvet,* Andy Hardy's favorite crush—Elizabeth Taylor—who boomed it out in *Boom* in 1968. It soon became as natural as gunfire in action flicks like *The French Connection.* President Nixon, however, was one of many Americans shocked to come across "that word" in the otherwise lovable *Love Story,* and many Americans were even more hurt to hear it turn up with considerable frequency in the Watergate tapes three years later.

Some say that the repeated use of four-letter words, by breaking old taboos, liberates us from their spell. Others say that words are subversive weapons, and to overuse them is to defuse them of their power. Still others point to the fall of Rome.

In the summer of 1968, at the time that President Nixon was coining the phrase "Peace with honor," a student at Wellesley, Massachusetts, was trying to explain the derivation of "that word" to townspeople outraged by its use in Leroi Jones's play *The Slave.* He was struggling to tell them that it merely comes from an archaic German agricultural verb *flicken,* which means "to plant seeds," and throughout time it eventually became *fuck,* meaning "to plant human seeds."

But the crowd did not hear him. They turned into a mob. And used the word *kill.* "Kill him," they shouted. "Kill him!"

So change, both in movies and in life, can be good or bad, depending on your point of view. Pornography is a frontier phenomenon, and obscenity is something you know when you see or hear it.

Too much change, however, coming too fast and too soon, can shake and shatter even our most liberal beliefs, leaving many of us confused and concerned. And that's what's happening now.

On the sexual frontier, producers seem to have pushed the boundary lines out of sight. After the sexual explicitness of *Deep Throat,* one had to wonder what anyone could do for an encore. Necrophilia? That was soon shown in a movie called *Deep Sleep,* prosecuted in a New Jersey suburb not so much because of its theme but because the exteriors were shot in the town without a permit. Coprophilia (look it up)? Marcello Mastroianni, no less, associates himself with that trick in *Le Grande Bouffe.* Bisexuality? "It's all there in *Score:* male and female, female and female, male and male." Sadomasochism? "In *The Night Porter,* love means never having to say ouch!" Bestiality? A movie called *Animal Lover* actually played to standing-room-only crowds of human beings in gray-flannel suits in many mini-cinemas from coast to coast. (I always firmly believed in that line from Tennessee Williams' *The Night of the Iguana*—"Nothing human disgusts me." But I was shaken when I heard about that one. I also believe that anyone who keeps a German shepherd as an apartment pet is obscene.) What about sacrilege? Surely not sacrilege. "Starts Friday. *Him.* More taboo, but successful, is *Him,* which is undoubtedly the first film to depict *Him* engaging in sexual activity."

What can possibly happen next?

Perhaps, if we cool it, what happened in Denmark. When sexually explicit material is made easily available, a saturation point is eventually reached and interest subsides. To be sure, "to write a prostitute," like prostitution itself, has been and probably will be with us always, but the current craze is a cultural phenomenon, and phenomena are observable in a framework of time. *The Village Voice,* a bellwether for cultural mores, suggests a future fad in an article entitled "Celibacy, The New Frontier."

Meanwhile, back on the violent frontier, today's good guys, from Charles Bronson's vigilante to the ubiquitous

Billy Jack (described by another *Voice* writer as "a Christ figure who likes to kick ass"), make yesterday's bad guys look as vicious as Bert and Ernie on *Sesame Street*. *Bring Me the Head of Alfredo Garcia* is "not a picture for the queasy or those in favor of happiness." And so it goes. As this book goes to press, a movie called *The Streetfighter* will be spilling blood across the silver screen in ways never dared before, and a sequel will appear at about the same time this book reaches your hands. In the initial *Streetfighter,* the hero rips out enemies' eyeballs, sniffs his fingers, tears off a foe's testicles and holds them high to get a better look, and slowly peels off another villain's throat and pulls out his tonsils. A real laugher, *The Streetfighter* is the first film so brutal that it is rated X for violence alone. But if the X threshold has expanded to make room for *The Streetfighter,* we can only wonder how much farther the lower ratings will widen to allow the now acceptable heroes like *Billy Jack* to kick, stomp, and mutilate enemies in the name of virtue. On the violent frontier, anything can happen next.

Only one thing is certain. And that is change.

Pornography is a frontier phenomenon, encompassing specific material considered out-of-bounds by a specific culture at a specific time. It is that one step beyond, simply by power of position, that stirs the senses and causes controversy.

And it may soon be the turn of violent movies to be considered out-of-bounds. But before we put on our helmets, let's put on our shades and see what lurks behind the blue door.

REEL TWO

Sex in the Movies

"It's even better when you help."
—LAUREN BACALL, in *To Have and Have Not*

In a nostalgic 1956 movie, *The Bachelor Party,* Don Murray, Jack Warden, and E. G. Marshall sit in a smoky apartment watching stag movies steam on a wall. You are not allowed to see what they see, but you do get to see their faces —and their reactions are worth a thousand reels.

Ten years later, Prof. Ira Carmen writes a classic textbook on movies and censorship, though he makes it clear from the start that stag films, of course, fall "beyond the purview of this investigation. Such materials are pornographic and are never shown publically."

Today, Murray, Warden, Marshall, Carmen, and you can go to New York or Dallas, San Francisco or Dayton, or almost any city at all, and watch a stag movie in a broken-down theater that used to show *Gone with the Wind.*

Hundreds of enterprising filmmakers, working in converted garages or with hand-held cameras in forest preserves, have churned out more than four thousand sex films between 1970 and today. In 1970, a hundred adult theaters in Los Angeles alone had to change their programs once a week to please the crowds.

In 1971, *Anomalies,* a dubious documentary about transvestites, fetishists, and sadomasochists, no doubt grossed out a lot of curiosity seekers, but it also grossed in more than $2 million in 128 cinemas from coast to coast.

In 1972, *The Stewardesses* took off on a nationwide tour that would eventually sell $25 million worth of tickets to porno passengers from Boston to San Diego.

And in 1973, two daringly different sex films, *Deep Throat* and *The Devil in Miss Jones,* climbed close to the top of the box-office charts, outdrawing some of the biggest Hollywood hopes of the year. "What we proved," says director Gerard Damiano, "is that you can go out and for $25,000 you can make $3 million rather than the majors spending $3 million to make $25,000." They also proved that Americans will pay for almost anything as long as it's "new."

In fact, *Deep Throat,* made as a lark in one week, took in $35,000 in its first week at a New York theater, went on to play in more than seventy other cities, and, before it was closed by law where it first began, had earned more than $5 million from its original $25,000 investment.

"But the thing that shocked me most about *Deep Throat,*" says Ned Tannen, vice-president of Universal Studios, "was that nobody in the audience wore a raincoat."

It's a rainy morning in Manhattan.

Below Times Square, you squeeze your way out of a subway, pull up the collar of your raincoat, and climb the Golgotha of stairs to the street. You are here to see your first dirty movie.

It's a twilight sort of morning and the only glimmer comes from the neon glare of movie marquees. Cars move slowly down 42d Street and you watch the falling mist through their yellow beams. On the corner, an old newsy warms his hands over a fire that burns in a garbage can. The flame isn't high enough to light a cigar and he rubs his hands like mad. "You wanna screw?" he asks.

"Huh? What do you mean?"

"You wanna *Screw!* They just come in. Over there. Pick one up."

Obediently, you step over to the newsstand. Next to a pile of *Wall Street Journal*s, sexual tabloids are spread out in a row like playing cards dealt by the Cincinnati Kid. *Pleazure, San Francisco Ball, Pussy, Hooker,* and *Screw.* You screw your courage to the sticking post and pick up the dealer's choice.

Screw—The Sex Review. An erotic drawing of a woman who is dripping what appears to be molten lava from between her legs adorns the cover. Above the drawing, red letters spell out the pleasures within: "Shaved Stripper from Sodom . . . Babes in Bondage . . . New Potions for Potency." You flip through the pages until you come to the movie reviews. In order to be selective, you must first study a diagram of an erect penis shooting sideways; underneath it, numbers run from ten to one hundred. It is the Peter Meter, a barometer for rating raunchy movies. Today's penis only makes it to 80, indicating that the current candidate cannot shoot par. You turn the page and run your finger down a listing of sex theaters in the area. And your eyes spin when they spot the following:

> "*CAMEO: 8th Ave. at 44th St. (246-9550), is a comfortable theater that usually shows high quality hardcore movies. This is one of the better show places for 16mm entertainment. Admission $5.*"

A movie buff, you know that the Cameo was once a showcase for Russian art films, and that Serge Eisenstein, director of such classics as *Potemkin,* beamed with pride in 1930 as photogs snapped his picture in front of the marquee. You drop the tabloid and head for the Cameo.

Down 42d Street you wind your way through the crowd, past adult bookstores with their windows painted black, past black women in doorways with their faces painted red, and past white teen-agers with Clearasil faces, who lean against lampposts and toss you come-hither looks. At Eighth Avenue you turn right, pass the Psychedelic Burlesk show, the Leisure Spa massage parlor, and a Christian Booksellers shop with copies of *The Total Woman* displayed in the window. At 44th Street, you cross the street against the red light, and stand in front of the Cameo. The marquee that once displayed Eisenstein's *Old and New* now spells out "All New! Direct from San Francisco. 16mm loops."

A gentle old lady who looks like your grandmother sits behind the ticket booth. Without looking her in the eye, you pull out five dollars, and push your way through the turnstile in the hope of trading your guilt for an hour or so of pleasure.

In the lobby, you are immediately denied the pleasure of popcorn. You enter the auditorium. The feature hasn't started yet, but the manager shamelessly keeps the lights on. The theater is scattered with men, and all of them stare at their knees, as if preparing for confession. You pick a seat on the side, away from everyone else, and wish you were someplace else.

On each side of the screen, a clock hangs on the wall. The clock on the left says 10:30. The one on the right says 2:15. You check your watch. It's almost twelve.

Hunched down, you look around and are surprised to see that most of the men are better dressed than you. They seem to be in their late thirties to mid-fifties, middle to upper middle class, and you can tell that they will go to their offices or make their sales calls and keep the economy rolling once the movie is over. At night, you can easily imagine them playing with their children, or coaching little league, or running programs for their local churches. Not one of them has a raincoat on his lap.

The lights dim. Thank God. The features begin.

For the next hour and a half, you are treated to one scratchy film after another that shows young men and women making love while Muzak pipes favorite themes by Mantovani. But there's no doubt about it. It is arousing. And fascinating. And oddly depressing. At one point, to your dismay, you think you are about to have an unusual accident. You remember a train ride you took as a teen-ager to a camp in Wisconsin. You and Jimmy Gibbons sat in a two-seater across from two Jesuit seminarians who were counselors. Jimmy fell asleep, his head against the window, but woke up in the middle of a wet dream. You laughed then. You're not laughing now. You turn your head from the sixty-foot screen and try to think of something else, anything—swimming, no, not swimming—climbing a tree, no, not that either—your images are symbols relating to what you have seen. But you manage to get control and eventually turn back to the screen.

It begins to get boring. There's something disconcerting about a twenty-foot phallus in close-up. It reminds you of the Washington Monument. One performer takes the place of another and after a while it's difficult to tell who is doing what to whom. You begin to look for little signs of individuality, anything that will personalize the performers and make them seem people with pasts: a butterfly tattooed on a girl's thigh, a St. Christopher medal swinging around a man's neck, an appendix scar, a chancre, hemorrhoids, anything—anything to hint who they are. Before you know it, the movies are done.

Several men jump from their seats and scamper for the exit. Others casually get up, stretch, and stroll up the aisle as if they've just seen *The Wizard of Oz*. You study their faces. Most seem to be dwelling on work they now must go and do. As you leave the theater, other men, much the same, file in.

The rain drives down sideways and splatters the sidewalk. You stand under the canopy and light a cigarette. You're not sure what to make of what you've seen, or even how you feel about it. One thing is sure: you don't feel like going out and raping anyone; in fact, you don't feel lustful at all. As the cold wind slaps your face, you feel about the same as when you came in, just a little melancholy, that's all. You know you'll tell your wife about it in a funny sort of way, but you also know that she'll see right through your humor and know that you're really covering up your embarrassment at being aroused by a movie and liking it. Why does that embarrass you? One thing is sure: if you make a joke out of pornography, you'll never be able to judge it maturely. But how do you judge it? Some say that it's a liberating experience, but you still feel inhibited, though some of the other men in the Cameo seemed pretty loose about it. Others say that pornography dehumanizes both the audience and the performers, but that assumes an omniscience about people they don't even know, and, besides, you don't feel any less human at all. Perhaps the odd sadness you feel makes you even more human. You think of Francis Thompson's line: "My heart sickens at all the sadness in the sweet, the sweetness in the sad." Is pornography sickening? Sad or sweet? Or perhaps a bit of them all. You have no easy answers.

But as you lean against the edge of the theater, in the same spot Sergei Eisenstein stood forty years ago, you do have one more question: "How in the hell did we get from there to here?"

In 1893, when Thomas Edison filmed a sneeze in New Jersey, and Fatima shook the Chicago Fair with her exotic *danse du ventre,* it was inevitable that the two events would one day come together. In the spring of the very next year, a squad of cops clomped down the Boardwalk of Atlantic City and busted a showing of *Dolorita and the Passion Dance*, thereby christening the first American film to cross a forbidden frontier. In those days, remember, navels stirred the senses.

Despite the bust, enterprising filmmakers smelled money and began to make daring movies in garages and in forest preserves. They threaded their finished films into little machines called nickelodeons. For a nickel, the viewer could peek into the machine and drool over reels like *Her Morning Exercise* in which a lady in tights does jumping jacks. Today, of course, nickelodeons are called "peep shows," and, inflation being what it is, the consumer now pays a quarter for every three minutes of a fifteen-minute "loop"—though what he sees is not what his grandfather saw. All five parts add up to $1.50, and the trick, I'm told, is to enter the peep show when the previous customer runs out of quarters at part five. That way, for only a quarter, you get the climax all to yourself.

At the turn of the century, not only were nickelodeons considered dangerous but so were the neighborhoods in which they played, also proving that the more things change, the more they stay the same. Legitimate theaters, showing comedies like *Princess Nicotine*, hung up neon signs that winked, "Electric Theatre, Moral and Refined, Pleasing to the Ladies." Across the ocean, a German artist prophesied: "We stand at the threshold of an altogether new art . . . which can stimulate our souls so deeply as only the tones of music have been able to." And when D. W. Griffith made *Birth of a Nation* in 1915, that art form was born. Stag films went underground, where they would stay until the late '60s.

Sex would, of course, be a movie theme from 1915 to the present. It's a fundamental, fascinating, and feeling-pitched human concern. But before the sixties, it was usually treated in subtle, suggestive, and seductive ways. For decades sex was synonymous with romance. Whether or not yesterday's filmmakers were inhibited by strict production codes or inspired by a love of narrative art that now seems nostalgic, or both, their movies teased instead of told all. "The problem with movies lately," says film critic Roger Ebert, "is that they're not content to tempt our innocence with a come-hither smile from a Marilyn or a Clark. They grab our innocence and run with it."

Oddly enough, the race to raunch began with the most innocent movie of all, *The Garden of Eden,* a 1954 documentary about nudism, shot in Florida and picked up by a distributor who tried to play it in New York. The movie was a wholesome reflection of the back-to-nature philosophy of social nudism, an oft suspected but generally accepted custom in Western civilization for centuries. The New York Department of Education, however, after previewing the film, found its nudity obscene. Ironically, nudity had been shown in African documentaries for years, but this was the first time that *white* bodies were bared. In movies like *Goona Goona* and *Bali,* brown and black nymphs, bare from the waist up, sashay with bowls of fruit on their heads like Carmen Mirandas without original sin. The public moralists never complained then, implying that black breasts are clean but that white ones are obscene.

The New York distributor took his *Garden of Eden* into the courtroom. In a landmark decision, Judge Charles Desmond ruled that "nudity in itself, and without lewdness or dirtiness, is not obscenity in law or in common sense." The movie was allowed to play. And it was a smash.

It wasn't long before enterprising filmmakers searched the forest preserves for nudist colonies. They were disappointed to find that most genuine nudists were middle-aged with sagging breasts and pockmarked buttocks. So they hired a bevy of models instead for a hundred dollars a day and all the free sun they could get, and went on to make phony nudies like *The Bare Hunt, The Barest Heiress, My Bare Lady,* and *Goldilocks and the Three Bares.* To keep it honest, a narrator would mouth platitudes about nudism while the models bruised their breasts in games of volleyball. There was no touching, no teasing, and, above all, no leering below the waist. Breasts and buttocks had edged over the frontier, but private parts were still out-of-bounds. Those volleyball games were well rehearsed.

The nudies of the '50s had two basic plots. In one, a voluptuous older woman invites a voluptuous younger one to join her at the nudist colony. The younger one blushes, bats her eyelashes, and confesses, "I'm shy." "Try it," soothes the older, "you'll like it." They arrive at the camp, enter separate cabanas, and slowly, oh so slowly, strip to the buff while Muzak pipes favorite themes by Mantovani. That's the good part. The rest of the movie degenerates into a naked *Sports Illustrated* featuring ping-pong, water polo, mountain-climbing, and baseball, in which the models, understandably, never slide home.

The other plot involves an investigative reporter doing a story on nudism for his paper. Fully dressed, pencil in hand, and sweat on brow, he listens to the lovelies equate sunshine with health, and volleyball with theology. By the end of the movie, he knows that they have ultimate truth and, like the blind man in the Gospel, he throws off his clothes and jumps into the pool. Distributors flooded the grind houses with nudies for four years.

By 1958, however, breasts and buttocks, even in technicolor, had about as much power to stir the senses and cause controversy as navels did in 1898. It was time for something "new."

In 1958, Russ Meyer, a onetime cheesecake photographer and combat cameraman in Korea, was out of work and looking for a way to put both his skills together. The result was *The Immoral Mr. Teas,* the most notorious frontier film to blush the face of America until *I Am Curious (Yellow)* would turn the country blue a decade later.

Mr. Teas is a buffoon in baggy pants who likes to daydream about girls. He would have made a great first baseman for the early New York Mets. One day Mr. Teas goes to the dentist, inhales too much anesthesia, and, from that moment on, every girl he sees—in offices, restaurants, on beaches—suddenly turns nude. To keep it moral, Meyer has Mr. Teas pleasantly ashamed of his magic. In fact, once he feels so guilty after watching three naked ladies cavort in a stream that he runs into a forest preserve. Where he proceeds to run into three more naked ladies. Desperate, Mr. Teas seeks help from a psychiatrist. Naturally, she's a woman, and just as the therapy begins to jell, her clothes vanish too. As the movie ends, a narrator intones, "Some men would just rather be sick."

The difference between *Mr. Teas* and the nudies is that in Meyer's film, the nudity takes place in the context of everyday life. Added to this is a whimsical narration, a bouncy musical score (on accordion), and first-rate photography.

The nudie cutie was born.

And it too was a smash. A 1960 Los Angeles *Times* notice said, "Last Friday evening the Peep Show finally moved across the tracks from Main Street, and to judge by the concourse of solid looking citizens, presumably all 18 or over, the film is going to be a GREAT success."

But if *Mr. Teas* was to become the father of *I Am Curious (Yellow)* and the grandfather of *Deep Throat,* he first had to sire the illegitimate births of hundreds of little tea bags—nudie cuties like *Not Tonight, Henry, Wild Gals of the Naked*

West, The Adventures of Lucky Pierre, and *Bachelor Tom Peeping,* a nudie cutie in which Francis Ford Coppola, later the director of *The Godfather,* first learned how to use a light meter.

The typical nudie cutie plot is exemplified in *Sinderella and Her Golden Bra,* in which the handsome prince, instead of picking up a fallen slipper, finds a Maidenform D Cup bra. He goes on to have every maiden in his kingdom, from A to D, try it on for size until he finds his Sinderella. He never touches them, and never even hints that he might desire them. He simply ogles. Arthur Knight and Hollis Alpert wrote in *Playboy,* 1967, that "the voyeuristic nature of these early nudies is perhaps the most striking thing about them. The hero does not crave sex; he just wants to look." They sound like they're describing *Playboy.*

Looking back on the age of the nudie cuties, film historians Kenneth Turan and Stephen F. Zito write, "It was the golden age of soft-core erotic fantasy, an innocent time during which movies showed all but the Real Thing." The real thing was not far behind. By the early '60s, nudity was no longer a novelty, even in Cinemascope. America was ready for something "new."

And what it got was a plot.

At the same time that Russ Meyer was teasing older adults, foreign films were pleasing younger adults. College students, in particular, found something in foreign movies they generally could not see in Hollywood films—a mixture of realism, metaphysics, and subtitles. So, while foreign directors had been making quality films for a long time, they suddenly became box office, and along came Bergman from Sweden, Truffaut from France, Fellini from Italy, and Kurosawa from Japan.

But some American distributors who couldn't tell a

Picasso from a Walter Keane used these films as if they were shot in garages or in forest preserves. A drive-in movie in Virginia played Fellini's *La Dolce Vita* as the second feature in a double feature with *Platinum High School.* Another distributor took Ingmar Bergman's *Monika,* a piercing story of a troubled adolescent, and retitled it *The Story of a Bad Girl.* Many theaters advertised the movies in such a way as to play up the erotic content without deemphasizing the artistic handling of it in order to have two cakes in one.

Rashomon, directed by Akira Kurosawa in 1951, was re-released in the early '60s as both an award winner and a movie with an explicit rape scene. When I was about twenty, I went to see it at the Capri theater, no doubt for both aesthetic and carnal reasons. But when I left the Capri, my head was filled not with sexuality at all but with epistemology—the meaning of truth.

In *Rashomon,* Toshiro Mifune plays a sweaty samurai who kills a nobleman and rapes his wife while a frightened woodcutter watches from behind a tree. The scene is told four times, from the points of view of each of the protagonists —the samurai, the nobleman, the wife, and the woodcutter —and the result is not only four different and contradictory stories, but a realization that all are both true and false, and that the truth of any experience depends on one's point of view. Objectivity may be an impossibility—which, of course, is also one of the themes of this book. In any event, anyone who saw *Rashomon* for any reason at all surely got more than he or she bargained for.

Ingmar Bergman's *The Virgin Spring* was another film that showed rape in a graphic but unsalacious way, and perhaps many people going to that movie received their first religious experience in cinema. The story comes from a four-teenth-century legend whose theme is the abundant love of God and the miracle of reconciliation. Bergman wrote at the time, "Our whole existence is based on the fact that there are things we may do and others that we may not do, and these are the complications that we constantly come into contact throughout our life." Which is another way of looking at the paradox of pornography.

Along with the wheat from across the oceans also came plenty of chaff. *And God Created Woman,* a suggestive movie with Brigitte Bardot that now seems sentimental, also made $4 million on American shores and begat *Mademoiselle Striptease,* who begat *The Twilight Girls,* who begat *The Weird Lovemakers,* who begat *Nights of Nymphomania*—all of which begat big money for importer Radley Metzger who went on to direct plush erotica like *Carmen Baby, I, a Woman,* and *Therese and Isabelle,* impelling the distinguished *Film Comment* journal to knight him "The Aristocrat of the Erotic."

Independent American producers, now working in penthouses from their profits on the nudies, made their versions of European films. Russ Meyer was the first to lead the pack with *Lorna,* an enormously successful film in which a heroine with breasts like watermelons marries a man with the sexual drive of a prune. Luckily, she runs into an escaped convict in a forest preserve and he rapes her. Together they come back to the shack in order to advance their plot, but the husband comes back and wipes them out. A melancholy "man of God" who looks like an extra from a Bergman film sermonizes, to keep it honest, that those who live by their swords will die by their swords. Shot in a moody black and white, like European films of the time, *Lorna* did have a primitive quality of art to it and played in theaters that never would have shown *Mr. Teas.*

But Lorna too gave birth to hundreds of little Lornas and again it wasn't long until the market was glutted. Breasts and buttocks, sweating and sighing, even in black and white, were no longer "new."

In 1969, a radical Swedish writer named Vilgot Sjöman made a movie to attack what he felt was the obscenity of the Swedish Welfare State and society in general. To counterbalance the alienation, acquisitiveness, and loneliness he found in modern Sweden, he filmed explicit scenes of give-and-take sex in casual, comic, and warmhearted ways. In one deliciously subversive scene, the young couple make love on the balustrade of the Royal Palace in front of a frozen but perspiring guard. The film was the next step beyond. Its name was *I Am Curious (Yellow)*.

And if it didn't take a year of battling with censors for the film to be allowed to be shown, few Americans would have bothered to see it. But after a year of talk and no show, it had become a celebrity. In a landmark case, the movie was declared to have "significant redeeming social values" and it went on to play at the Evergreen theater in New York. Lines stretched down 11th Street and up University Place to Union Square. But many of those who got in to see it at last didn't sit through until the end. The movie really did have "redeeming social value"—it was a socialist manifesto—and the sex scenes were a minor part of the whole.

But by crossing another forbidden frontier, *I Am Curious (Yellow)* led the movie moguls to ask: "If that movie is making money because of its explicit sexuality, why not make movies that show the same but don't bore audiences at the same time?"

It wasn't long until 20th Century Fox asked Russ Meyer to direct a multimillion dollar sexploitation film, *Beyond the Valley of the Dolls,* and other major studios got bolder but still stopped short of showing the "real thing." The simulated sexuality was as well rehearsed as the volleyball games of the early nudies.

Meanwhile, younger Russ Meyers, working in motels, began making beaver films and showing them in peep shows and converted garages called mini-cinemas. Instead of a woman in tights doing jumping jacks, in a beaver, a nude woman lies on a bed and does leg raises, spreading them as they get high. Though these were a sensation for a few months, once viewers learned what a variety of vaginas looked like they were either sated, satisfied, saddened, or all three.

In the grind houses that used to show *Mr. Teas,* the key phrase was now "socially redeeming value." *Censorship in Denmark* was a pseudo documentary that spliced in home-made hard-core footage with a travelogue of liberated Denmark. It gave birth to movies like *Censorship USA, Pornography USA, Sexual Liberty Now,* and *Pornorama.* All employed the old technique of a moralistic narration while showing every manner of sexual technique.

A History of the Blue Movie pieced together old stag movies with new ones under the guise of research, and proved that not only is there a way around censorship but that the old-timers made better erotic movies than the new-timers. This approach was repeated in *Hollywood Blue, Making the Blue Movie,* and *Pornography in Hollywood.*

Educational films like *The Art of Marriage, Lessons in Love,* and *Man and Wife* also appeared under the pretense of being filmed Masters-and-Johnson techniques for improving your marriage, though even the best of them looked like army training films.

But each, in their own way, could lay claim to socially redeeming value. Vincent Canby wrote in *The New York Times,* "My own experience is that some of the sequences in these new films are erotic, but it is a fleeting, certainly harmless kind of eroticism that depends largely on shock and curiosity which turns into an almost scholarly interest and then dwindles in a sort of arrogant boredom."

By the end of 1971, scholarly hard core was turning the

grind houses into unaccredited colleges of sex. Soon something would happen to change the scene again. A movie with no pretense at all would leap across what seemed to be the last frontier.

There may be a sucker born every minute, but a Linda Lovelace comes along only once in a blue movie.

Up until *Deep Throat* played at the New Mature World Theater on 49th Street, that movie house, like the Harem, the Doll, and the Eros theaters, all bordering Times Square like prostitutes, served the needs of middle-aged men. What was new about *Deep Throat* was not what it showed on the screen, but who sat in front of the screen. Husbands and wives, secretaries and diplomats, singles, swingles, and retirees. *The New York Times* reported limousines pulling up to the curb of the New Mature World Theater and dropping off such celebrities as Truman Capote, Sandy Dennis, Mike Nichols, and Jack Nicholson. The Russian Olympic Basketball Team tried to get in, but had only rubles. The Los Angeles *Free Press* alleged that Frank Sinatra arranged a private showing for Spiro Agnew. A Hollywood producer supposedly had a special screening for Henry Kissinger in a palace not far from San Clemente.

The public and the press gave more attention to this 61-minute movie than to a lengthy report from the Club of Rome that half the world was starving to death.

Vincent Canby called it "junk." Mort Sheinman, in *Woman's Wear Daily,* said, somewhat tongue in cheek, that it was a "remarkable film" that "provides a bold thrust forward in the history of contemporary cinema, plunging deeply into areas seldom, if ever, explored on screen. . . . All in all, a rare treat." Nora Ephron, writing in *Esquire,* felt that "not to have seen it seemed somehow derelict," but found it "one of the most unpleasant, disturbing films I have

ever seen—it is not just anti-female, but anti-sexual as well."
Kevin Sanders of WABC television was pleased and went on
to become television's only movie reviewer to regularly discuss hard-core films. *Screw*'s Peter Meter rated it 100%.
Ellen Willis in *The New York Review of Books* found it
"about as erotic as a tonsillectomy." "Where is the charm?"
asked Andrew Sarris in *The Village Voice*. "Where is the
humor? Where is the eroticism? Where is the liberation?
Finally, where is the exit?"

Who was right and who was wrong? The samurai? The
nobleman? The wife? The woodcutter? Or all of them?

Your baby-sitter has a sore throat.

But that's O.K. She doesn't talk much anyway. You pull
into the tree-shaded driveway of your home. The baby-sitter
hops out and your wife jumps in. You slide back out into the
street. You are going to see your first dirty movie together:
Deep Throat.

It's an October-like evening for late August, and a warm
breeze blows yellow leaves across the road as you drive toward Stamford, Connecticut.

The downtown suburb is a sleepy area even on a Friday
night, so it should be easy to find a place to park. You pass
one of the four shows in town. A dozen teen-agers line up like
scrubs to get into *The Longest Yard.*

"That's one I'd really like to see," you say. "It sounds real
good."

"Is that the one with Burt Reynolds?" your wife asks.

"Right."

"I'd like to see it too."

"I hear it's not so hot."

She picks up the folded newspaper on the seat and opens
it to the movie section. "Too late," she says. "It started
already. But listen." She reads the advertisement. " '*The*

Longest Yard . . . an avalanche of brutalizing fury. The effect is jarring, numbing and brutalizing. It's violent and it's nitty gritty and raw. What more do you want in these angry times? You are so carried away that you don't have time to think.' "

"I told you it was good."

"Sounds awful. Will we be late for the other one?"

"We'll just make it." You turn the corner. The street the show is on looks like a Detroit assembly line. Every parking place is filled. You remember *The Great Gatsby* and how everybody just *had* to see it, even though everybody else told them it really wasn't very good. A multimillion-dollar advertising campaign had much to do with that. How much does the free publicity from cops and courts have to do with the rage over *Deep Throat*?

You're in luck. A Pontiac tank pulls out from right in front of the Plaza and you slip your little Opel in like a penny in a nickelodeon.

A teen-ager in a Levi suit hassles the lady in the ticket booth. "I *am* 21," he says.

"You don't look it," she says, "do you have an ID?"

"I left it at home," he says.

"Then go back home and get it. You can't get in without it. I'm sorry."

The kid mumbles a curse word and stalks away.

You buy two tickets, only three bucks apiece, and enter the theater. The Plaza is clean, but it's seen better days. At one time it showed family movies but perhaps was losing money since fewer people left their homes to see movies they could see for free on television. You can barely make out the Oriental pattern on the threadbare carpet, a standard in cinemas not so long ago. The candy counter is a Christmas stocking made of glass and steel. "Do you want some popcorn?" you ask. Your wife thinks it over. "No," she says. "It doesn't seem right." You buy yourself an Almond Joy.

Hand in hand, you enter the auditorium and walk down the slanted aisle. The theater is almost filled. Most people pack the middle section, strangers rubbing shoulders with strangers, as if they are about to see just another movie. You find two seats off to the side.

Both of you look around. Is that your dentist and his wife in the front row? Your wife points out someone from the Junior League on the other side. You spot three men who ride the rails to the city with you each morning. All are apparently with their wives. And all of them spot you.

The lights dim. The curtain parts. The show begins.

A freckle-faced girl with fluffy hair drives down a Miami street in a blue sports car. A rock group sings, "Deep Throat, don't row a boat, don't get your goat, that's all she wrote, Deep Throat." The words do not inspire. But the music is bright and strong. Credits appear beneath the girl's face. She is Linda Lovelace. At the end of the credits, Linda alights from the car and seems to float down the street like a fragile butterfly. You recall the scene in *Billy Liar* in which Julie Christie first hypnotized an audience by strolling down a street and casually swinging a purse. Linda doesn't cast that same kind of spell at all, but she does have a mild sort of magic in what appears to be total unselfconsciousness.

Linda enters a suburban house where she encounters her roommate Helen sitting on a kitchen counter. Helen draws up her legs and a delivery boy performs cunnilingus. "Do you mind if I smoke while you're eating?" she asks the boy. A few people in the audience twitter nervously. "That's not funny," your wife says. "I know," you say gravely.

The boy leaves. Linda tells Helen that she has a problem: she enjoys sex, too, but is disappointed because she never has an orgasm. "I want to hear bells ringing, dams bursting, rockets exploding," Linda says. Helen suggests that she try something new. "Different strokes for different folks, you know?" Who wrote this, you wonder, Rowan and Martin?

Helen calls up about a dozen of her boyfriends. They all come over to help ring Linda's bell. The next scene has everything you saw at the Cameo, with one remarkable exception. Linda Lovelace is really enjoying herself. And that helps you enjoy it too. Doesn't she know there's a camera and four klieg lights in front of her? She sure doesn't seem to mind. She is happy in her work. "I can't believe this," you whisper to your wife.

"Hypocrite. Hush up and chew your Almond Joy."

At first the audience is very quiet for this scene, a little shocked perhaps, but it soon becomes apparent that nothing that follows can be any more shocking, and you soon sense a relaxation in yourself and in the audience. You've seen all there is to see, and it's time to either leave or just sit back and see what happens next. No one leaves.

The scene ends. Linda's bells still haven't rung. More depressed than ever, she consults a psychiatrist. And he discovers that her problem is not in her head but inside her neck. Linda's clitoris is located deep in her throat. Now she feels worse than ever.

"It's not so bad," he soothes her. "You should be thankful you have a clitoris at all."

"That's easy for you to say," Linda sobs. "How would you feel if your balls were in your ears?"

"Why, then I could hear myself coming!" he exclaims.

An expected wave of laughter ripples through the theater. It's the kind of vulgar joke that many men tell to each other on commuter trains and later tell to their wives, even though they always heard it from someone else, of course. The difference now is that the joke is in a movie, and, with three hundred people sharing it, it somehow seems less crude.

To make Linda's life more comfortable, the doctor teaches her a special way of fellatio. And the rest of course is history.

You are aroused, to be sure, but most of the action is taking place in your head. "How on earth does she do it?" At the end of the scene, bells ring, bombs blast, and fireworks splash the screen. You wonder if the director borrowed from Alfred Hitchcock who did pretty much the same thing after Cary Grant and Grace Kelly kiss in *To Catch a Thief.*

The movie goes on.

And on.

And on and on.

Linda reaches total happiness at the conclusion when she falls in love with a young athlete whose penis is as big as a Louisville Slugger. A wag in front of you whispers, "I can't believe she ate the whole thing." Rockets explode. It is the end.

The lights go on. Everyone casually gets up and heads up the aisles. Wives talk to husbands. Friends talk to friends. You listen to what they say. Some felt disgust. Others thought it was funny. Several people say, "Now I know. I've seen enough." And they laugh. Like you and your wife, they will now go home, pull up the blankets on their sleeping children, kiss their foreheads, and then watch television or talk or maybe make love.

Driving home in the dark, your wife hunched close to you, you ask her, "Did you think it was obscene?"

"It was dirty all right."

"Did it bother you?"

"What do you mean?"

"Did it upset you? I mean, make you feel—you know, yucchy."

"The kids' diapers make me feel yucchy. No, it wasn't so bad. But I'd rather see *Wuthering Heights.*"

"Was it sexy?" you ask.

"It was to you," she answers.

"How do you know?"

"Your hand was sweaty." Both of you laugh.

"Well, what about you?" you want to know.

"That's for me to know," she says with a smile. "And for you to find out."

You dwell on that for a moment. "One last question," you ask. "Do you think *Deep Throat* has socially redeeming value?"

"Not a bit. Are you kidding?" She pauses a moment, then asks, "But what's socially redeeming about *I Love Lucy*?"

Later on, after kissing the children in their sleep, you share a pitcher of hot chocolate and talk about many things. And soon enough, you do what married people who love each other often do.

And it is something good.

Deep Throat is, of course, as different from the Cameo loops as the novel *Candy* is from a telephone book, but one could, if one wished, still argue that it is obscene, no matter how you define the term, and no matter who goes in to see it.

Lawyer Richard Kuh is one of many critics who argue that such "pornography is one-dimensional. It presents seductive shadows, not people." Baptist psychologist John Drakeford calls it "a sexual mirage." In other words, movies like *Deep Throat,* by showing only a part of human sexuality as if it were the whole, distort sexual values. *Deep Throat,* the argument goes, degrades sex by emphasizing the genital aspect and ignoring the affective. Surely there is more to human sexuality than clanging bells and shooting stars. Such a misrepresentation is dehumanizing and obscene.

I can buy that argument myself. Intellectually. But to be balanced about it, I'd have to apply that basic principle behind the blue door to movies that play in front of the blue door as well.

Why don't we pose the same principle to family films that misrepresent the family, marriage, politics, war, or even religion? If you wanted to be fair and rigorously scientific, you could also describe a pornography of piety.

Simply apply the principle to Biblical epics, with their casts of Yugoslavian thousands, like *The Robe, The Prodigal, Sodom and Gomorrah, Salome,* and *The Bible* itself, starring John Huston as a zany zoo keeper named Noah. Could we not call these movies "religious mirages"? But we don't. Why not?

How many times has God been disguised as a soldier in movies like *A Wing and a Prayer* and *God Is My Copilot?* In the latter, Flying Tiger ace Dennis Morgan confesses to a priest that he's slaughtered a hundred Japs that day and feels sick about it. The priest mumbles a platitude and makes him feel good. Can't such a one-dimensional view of God be interpreted as a "divine mirage"?

The Son of God, of course, has been more distorted in movies than Billy the Kid. Jeffrey Hunter plays him as a divine weakling with shaved armpits in the 1961 *King of Kings,* also known as *I Was a Teen-age Jesus.* In that movie, the real hero is Barrabas, a nice guy whom Jesus lets down, just as the real hero of the rock opera *Jesus Christ Superstar* is Judas, a caring person whom Jesus also fails. Max von Sydow is a very human Jesus who has trouble keeping his wig on in *The Greatest Story Ever Told* in 1965, shot in Utah because it looks more like Palestine than Palestine, and starring a galaxy of Hollywood stars, including John Wayne as a centurion in a steel cowboy hat who certainly woke me up when he stabbed Jesus in the side and drawled, "This sure was the Son of God." In Pasolini's realistic *The Gospel According to St. Matthew,* Jesus is a communist. In *Godspell,* he is a clown. And, in many of Luis Buñuel's films, he is a pervert. Surely, one or more of these movies misrepresents

Jesus, shows only one side of his reality—divine or human, strong or weak, beautiful or ugly—and is each in its own way a "Christological mirage."

The same principle can be applied to many of Christ's emissaries—Fathers Bing Crosby, Pat O'Brien, and Spencer Tracy, to name one trinity. Please don't get me wrong. I catch *Going My Way* every Thanksgiving on television, and tears still squeeze out of the corners of my eyes every time Barry Fitzgerald waddles toward his ancient mother as the movie ends. I love them all. All I'm saying is that these movies too present seductive shadows, not real people, are one-dimensional in their treatment of religion, and could be called "religious mirages," depending on your point of view. James Agee, reviewing *Going My Way* in 1944, wrote: "Strictly speaking, this hardly has a right to pose as a religious film. There is no real contest with evil or with suffering, and the good itself loses half its force, because even the worst people in *Going My Way* are as sugar-coated as Mrs. Wiggs of the Cabbage Patch." If you also recall, the most crucial moral problem in *The Bells of St. Mary's* is the best way to teach a kid to box.

I'll never forget Otto Preminger's hymn to the collection plate, *The Cardinal,* in 1963. Father Tom Tyron fights and licks the Ku Klux Klan and Hitler's Germany, small-town gossips and the hierarchy itself, but his biggest and most unbelievable victory is keeping his hands off Romy Schneider, who pursues him around the globe. Talk about a "sexual mirage."

James Agee summed up most so-called religious movies for *The Nation* in 1945: "I am," he wrote, "getting a little tired of seeing movies thought of as 'religious' which carry not much more religious meaning or insight or adventurousness than a bourgeois' good intentions at New Years. Not that priests would be by any means necessary to a good

religious picture. I can't help noticing that they never yet
have been shown on the screen at their real business, public
or private; just as screen lovers are seldom shown to be
capable of love."

Yes, *Deep Throat* misrepresents human sexuality because
the characters there too seem incapable of love. And I'm sure
that every adult in the Plaza saw right through that mirage
as they see through other mirages in other acceptable films.

So *Deep Throat* is junk.

What else is new?

If one argues that the pornography of piety is tasteless or
obscene, that doesn't make the pornography of sex any less
so. The latter may even be more so or not at all so, depending
on your point of view.

But if one argues that movies about Jesus can transcend
tastelessness simply by virtue of good intentions and thereby
escape the label of obscenity, one must in fairness apply that
principle in front of the blue door to those behind it.

In *Pornography and the Law,* Drs. Eberhard and Phyllis
Kronhausen make a distinction between *obscenity,* or what
we know as hard-core pornography, and *erotic realism,* or
what we know as the literature of sexuality.

In obscenity, the primary purpose is sexual stimulation,
and everything else, if there is anything else, is secondary. In
erotic realism, the primary purpose is the "honest portrayal
of man's sexual nature," and any sexual stimulation that
accompanies it is secondary.

Obscenity exploits sexuality. Erotic realism explores it.
The difference between the two is the difference between
Lady Chatterley's Lover and a raunchy rip-off in an adult
bookstore, called *Lady Chatterley's Chimpanzee.*

Dr. Anders Groth, a Danish psychiatrist, puts it this way:
"Good pornography is erotic art where people are people

with human feelings. Bad pornography is pornography where people act mechanically and where they have feelings only concerned with sex."

Psychiatrist Preben Hertoft argues, "If it is not against the law, you will get better pornography. It may be possible for people with talent to make some films that are artistic."

But such specific films may still offend the moral standards of a specific culture at a specific time. Peter Michelson, in *The Aesthetics of Pornography,* reminds us, however, that "no man, and certainly no artist, is obliged to have a moral vision that pleases us. His vision may not even please him. But when we penetrate the implications of dissident moralities we often find a reality that gives us profound moral knowledge whether or not we subscribe to *its* particular metaphysics."

One should, then, be able to talk about a *Last Tango in Paris* in terms of the artist's vision rather than in terms of "contemporary standards of propriety." The movie has a moral beneath and beyond, yet supported and enhanced by, its graphic montage. The sexual scenes are integral to the artist's "honest portrayal of man's sexual nature," whether or not one subscribes to "its particular metaphysics." If one can accept the validity of erotic realism, one can then go on to appreciate and evaluate *Last Tango* as one would any other exploration of another human experience. In *Last Tango,* pornography, albeit soft-core, transcends tastelessness by providing the ambience for a moral vision.

In Rip Torn's *Coming Apart,* directed by Moses Ginsberg in 1969, hard-core pornography becomes the medium for an artistic statement that seems to damn pornography itself. Torn plays a psychiatrist who hides a movie camera in a glass box. He puts the box on a coffee table that sits in the center of his room. He aims the camera at a sofa with a huge mirror behind it. Therefore, whoever is either in front of or in back of the camera gets photographed. Torn sets up sexual encounters in his apartment and later replays them for himself alone on a movie screen. Every variety of sexual experience takes place, masturbation, fellatio, intercourse, done first in passion, then indifference, and finally in coldness. Increasingly, Torn becomes more fascinated by what he sees on the screen than the realities those images represent. Gradually, Torn comes apart, and those who follow the narrative rhythm of the movie also get torn within as well as Torn on the screen. The movie is a Zen koan. The viewer is a voyeur watching a movie about a voyeur viewing a movie about himself. You are Torn, and Torn is you. The mirror in his room, smashed in despair at the end, symbolically reflects the screen in front of the audience. *Coming Apart* is an uneven but deeply unnerving movie that uses hard-core pornography to make a moral statement about both the characters on the screen and the characters who sit in front of the screen. It explores a hidden aspect of human sexuality and brings it out into the open with complexity, imagination, and nerve.

Both these movies, *Last Tango* and *Coming Apart,* prove that people with talent can make sexually explicit movies that are not only artistic but have a strong moral vision as well. Both are also exceptions that prove the rule. Distinguishing the wheat from the chaff in sex movies is often an exercise in the discernment of the spirits. What you've seen above and what you'll see below is simply one woodcutter's point of view.

You have your five dollars ready this time. *Memories Within Miss Aggie* is a hard-core film hailed by some critics as one of the most artistic within the genre. As you enter the theater, you do not know yet that the reason it is considered art is that it looks like it was shot on Ingmar Bergman's wintry island when he was off on an American tour. You do know that its director is Gerard Damiano, who also did *Deep Throat* and *The Devil in Miss Jones.* One reviewer has compared him to Alfred Hitchcock. You do know why. In *Miss Jones,* the heroine slashes her wrists while taking a bath, filling the tub with blood. The reviewer thought he was seeing *Psycho.* You also know that no one is allowed into this theater during the shocking conclusion of *Aggie.* And you also know better. Any adult with five bucks can get in anytime at all.

The theater is empty. You sit in the middle. You try to put aside your initial doubts and evaluate the movie on its own artistic terms.

Miss Aggie, a middle-aged spinster, lives on an isolated farm with a male companion who silently sits on a rocker and listens to her talk about how it used to be. She recalls, and you are allowed to see, three memories from Aggie's past. In each memory, Aggie is portrayed by a different performer, a blonde, a brunette, and a redhead, who with their male companions show you intercourse, sodomy, and fellatio. After the fellatio scene, done to a tune that builds to a climax like the beat of bolero, the movie is, for all intents and purposes, over.

But it continues. In the last memory, Aggie recalls, and you are allowed to see, how she met the man in the chair. She bumps into him as she is coming out of a church. She asks him to come over for some hot soup and to stay on through the cold dark night. "I'll come," he says. That night, Aggie steals into his bedroom. You glimpse a gleaming butcher knife held behind her back. It must be time for the "shocking conclusion." You are frightened. Not because of any built-up suspense but because you know if the ending is similar to the middle, you might be treated to a castration scene. Just what you need on a muggy day. You squirm. The man unbuttons his shirt. You squirm some more. He takes off his shirt and leans back with his eyes closed. Your heart pounds. You know how realistic special-effects men can make things look. Aggie raises the knife. Oh, my God. She plunges the knife—splotch!—into his eye. Blood pours down his face like a waterfall. And you are tremendously relieved. It wasn't as bad as you thought.

The movie ends with Aggie back in the present, talking to the figure in the chair. You now see that the head of the man is really a withered skull with a gaping hole where the eye socket should be. Were all those memories of sex merely fantasies? Have you just seen another pseudo *Psycho?* Or simply *The Devil in Miss Jones* all over again? The movie is over, and you rush out for some fresh air. By the time you hit the street, you forget what your questions were.

As I see it, if there is anything obscene about *Memories Within Miss Aggie,* it is not the sex, which is lusty and generally joyful, but rather that *the movie as a whole* pretends to be something it is not. It is a lie. The screenplay is nothing more than a phony framework for the three sexual set pieces, masquerading as ambiguous art. It explores nothing and seems to exploit everything. And considering the ugly finale, it seems to be a sex movie designed more to punish than to please. To use a bit of reverse logic, it is the explicit sexuality that gives redeeming value to *Memories Within Miss Aggie.*

What was at least refreshing about *Deep Throat,* in addition to the innocent enthusiasm of its star, was the movie's complete lack of guile. It was a locker-room joke made by adult adolescents for other adult adolescents, and it didn't pretend to be anything else.

And, finally, what distinguishes *Deep Throat* from *Last Tango* is that in the latter movie there is a connection between genitals and human minds and hearts. "Not even the most recognized methods of sexual intercourse," wrote that old rascal Havelock Ellis, "can well be recognized as aesthetic unless qualified by more specifically human emotions." That's why hard core has such a hard time being art. And that's why Marlon Brando refuses to take his underwear off. It would strip away his masculine mystique.

Apply the *Wuthering Heights* test to see what I mean. Emily Brontë's love story is one of the greatest of all time. And who can ever forget Laurence Olivier's brooding Heathcliff and Merle Oberon's fickle Cathy as they embrace each other on a mountain overlooking the moors, facing a bitter world they never made? Max Steiner's romantic score adds vibrancy to a love story that is doomed before it begins. Now imagine that scene being redone in hard core. Can you? A hard-core Heathcliff and a concupiscent Cathy? Olivier and Oberon grunting and groaning as a fierce Welsh wind whips their naked flesh? I can imagine it, but I'd rather not.

To be fair, however, we should also apply the *Don't Look Back* test. That particular 1974 movie with Julie Christie and Donald Sutherland was essentially an occult melodrama, but a key element in the film is the deep love shared by the married couple. And director Nicholas Roeg photographs an erotic love scene between Christie and Sutherland that is both explicit and exquisite, tasteful and integral to the plot, suggesting that such scenes could possibly form the nucleus of another specific movie about love.

"*Wet Rainbow,*" says Gay Talese, "is the first erotic movie about love." You are very weary of sex movies by now, but you will shell out a final fiver to see if *Wet Rainbow* passes the *Don't Look Back* test. The movie stars Georgina Spelvin, "The Helen Hayes of Hardcore," and Harry Reems, hairy veteran of hundreds of hard-core films, who is famed for his uncanny ability to ejaculate every time the director shouts, "Shoot." Both have legitimate theater background, and both can act when they're in the mood.

In *Wet Rainbow,* they play a married couple very much in love. They bump into a pretty young thing named Rainbow who sulks around in tight levis and a Mickey Mouse T-shirt. They still love each other. But now they both lust after Rainbow too. Despite a few histrionics, the movie does develop the theme at a deliberate pace, and while there is eventually plenty of explicit sex—between Harry and Georgina, Georgina and Rainbow, Rainbow and Harry, Harry and Rainbow and Georgina (are you following me?)—the movie does explore the love-lust mythos as well as exploit the prodigious talents of its stars. It is surely not the first sex film about love, but it is, in its own groping way, a love film with plenty of sex. And it may point to a time when a specific movie will combine the best of all the elements discussed above—explicit sex, artistry, vision, and love.

It's possible. Even probable. And maybe inevitable. But I'll tell you a secret. I won't go out of my way to see it. Frankly, after two months of seeing so many movies that promise or pretend to do just that, I've had enough. For me, the best argument against sexually explicit movies is that after a short time they simply lose their sex appeal. To be sure, they grab you by the groin and pull you into the action, but what's so very sexy about that?

You can see everything in movies today, but has there ever been a sexier striptease than that by the young girl at the end of the 1950 *Asphalt Jungle,* in which she doesn't take off a stitch of her clothes? Master criminal Sam Jaffe was so hypnotized that he forgot to make his getaway and got nabbed by the law. Film critic Roger Ebert argues that the sexiest striptease was performed by Rita Hayworth in the steamy 1946 melodrama *Gilda,* and I wouldn't argue too much with him except to say that Rita peels off only her gloves. You can hear everything in movies today, but has anyone ever spoken a sexier line than the young Lauren Bacall in the 1944 *To Have and Have Not* when, after giving a lingering kiss to Humphrey Bogart, she pulls back slowly and says in a low voice, "It's even better when you help"? I don't think so. And I wouldn't be surprised if most people agreed.

Sex in the movies has crossed a lot of frontiers since Dolorita first shimmied on celluloid in 1894, but don't be surprised if by the end of this decade, or sooner, the next step beyond will be a free and deliberate step behind.

Meanwhile, in both the public and the legal minds, sexual pornography is still synonymous with obscenity while other forms of obscenity are not considered pornography. Attorney Charles Rembar, in *The End of Obscenity,* paradoxically points out that obscenity is therefore "usually defined as lewd, lewd is defined as lascivious, lascivious as libidinous, libidinous as licentious, and licentious as lustful." It's a case of the snake eating its own tail.

And so we come full circle.

What makes a movie obscene?

Barry Goldwater, "as a father and a grandfather," knows it when he sees it.

And I, as a grandson and father, know it too.

But both of us, I'm sure, have different points of view.

And that's the paradox of pornography.

In 1968, President Lyndon Johnson established a commission to crack the paradox through massive research, exhaustive studies, and scientific testing into the nature, extent, and effects of sexual pornography. The commission was composed of leading lawyers and educators, scientists and artists, doctors and clergymen. Its members included Democrats and Republicans, liberals, conservatives, and all those in between. Two years and $2 million later, they delivered a historic and heavy 656-page document to President Richard

Nixon—The 1970 Report of the American Commission on Obscenity and Pornography.

In a highly detailed technical report, the Commission found no evidence linking sexual materials to sexual crimes, and, as offensive as such pornography may be to some, found no evidence that it has any deleterious effect on the character or moral values of either adults or adolescents. Because of insufficient research, children should not be exposed to such material, but all laws prohibiting the availability of sexually explicit material to consenting adults should be repealed.

Some people cheered the report. Others hissed. Most people went to the movies.

President Nixon, whose favorite movie at the time was *Patton,* rejected the report as "morally bankrupt." Those who cheered now hissed. The former hissers cheered. And most people went to the movies.

"If an attitude of permissiveness were to be adopted regarding pornography," said Mr. Nixon, "this would contribute to an atmosphere condoning anarchy in every other field —and would increase the threat to our social order as well as to our moral principles. . . . We all hold the responsibility for keeping America a good country. American morality is not to be trifled with."

A few members of the Commission released a minority report, also well-reasoned, that challenged and contradicted the conclusions of the majority. The Senate jumped on the bandwagon and declared that "the Commission has not properly performed its duties nor has it complied with the mandates of Congress." And Vice-President Spiro Agnew proclaimed, "So long as Richard Nixon is President, Main Street will not be turned into Smut Alley." By this time, almost everyone was going to the movies.

While only the most effete snob would claim that sexual pornography is necessary to liberate Main Street, only the most self-deceived person could believe that its prohibition would return Main Street to an innocence that never existed in the first place. Main Street was Peyton Place long before Linda Lovelace was born. And worse obscenities have taken place on Pennsylvania Avenue.

And if it were really obvious that sexual pornography led to sexual crimes, all Americans would want to ban both Doris Day and the devilish Miss Jones. But the only long-range data available comes from Denmark, where total lack of censorship of pornography for several years was accompanied by a *reduction* of sex-related crimes. Some psychologists say that the easy accessibility to such material can actually help *prevent* such crimes by easing sexual tensions. Actress Sarah Miles, learning that her movie *Lady Caroline Lamb* might be rated out-of-bounds for adolescents because her breasts are visible, made a comment that is flippant but not irrelevant: "I am amused that someone thinks that a glimpse of my nipples could corrupt the youth of America. When I read statistics like one in every five people in America is either burgled or mugged, I wonder whether a glimpse of nipple now and then might help." But no matter what celebrities or psychiatrists have to say either pro or con, the cultural phenomenon of the day is likely to remain a scapegoat for some time to come.

Some effective counterarguments to witch-hunting, however, can be gleaned from history. An Episcopal church study on the church's role in human sexual development points out some interesting facts: "In the first century, Martial blamed loose morals on horse racing and gladiatorial combats. In the sixteenth century, moralizers were blaming the troubadors. In eighteenth-century England, cheap novels were held to be the ruination of moral codes. Flaubert, a century ago, pointed scornfully at the vulgar periodicals flowing out of Paris. Then it was the Sunday supplements, movies, radio, and television. However, since the Payne

Foundation study of movies and children in the 1930's, not a single scholarly study of the impact of the media has supported these rather easy claims. Certainly, some individuals may intensify their baser nature by being exposed to mass-media communication, but it helps not at all to be content with this approach."

However, many people feel that it helps not at all to be content with the above approach, and are horrified that the American Commission on Obscenity, after two years and $2 million, declared that it would not be wise to "recommend any definition of what is obscene for adults." After all, don't we all know it when we see it?

The Rev. Howard Moody offered an interesting definition of obscenity in the magazine *Christianity and Crisis* during the civil rights movement of 1965. "For Christians, the truly obscene ought not to be slick-paper nudity, nor the vulgarities of dirty old or young literati, nor even 'weirdo' films showing transvestite orgies or male genitalia. What is obscene is that material, whether sexual or not, that has as its basic motivation and purpose the degradation, debasement and dehumanizing of persons." For Moody, the dirtiest words in the English language are not of the four-letter variety, but any racial epithet spat from the mouth of a bigot.

Of course, Moody's definition of obscenity—with its key words of "degradation, debasement and dehumanizing"—would be just as difficult to apply to specific material as are all the definitions handed down by the courts for a century —with their key words of "patently offensive" and "purient interest" and "community standards." But from this wood-cutter's point of view, it's the clearest personal guide I've ever seen in print.

On the one hand, I would not, of course, want my children to see *Deep Throat* or *Last Tango*, no matter which definition of obscenity I may choose to use. On the other hand, I would not like them to see *High Plains Drifter* either, a Clint Eastwood Western that features, in addition to rape, a brutal whipping. I am grateful that there is no way they can get into an X-rated movie even if they had five bucks. I am not particularly thrilled that movies like *High Plains Drifter* are now a staple on the *TV Movie of the Week*. But that's my problem, just as sex movies may be a problem for someone else, and I can handle it.

While there is no convincing proof that sexually explicit movies can produce harmful effects on young people, there is also no proof that they can do them any good either, and it's tough enough to pass through adolescence without being exposed to needless turbulence from without. At the same time, laws that would restrict the freedom of adults to see adult films for "the sake of the children" are a sham. It's like saying that the Government should be allowed to wiretap private citizens for "the sake of national security." Both instances lead to abuses, and both refuse to face the real issue. According to the Sex Information and Education Council, "the best protection of young people against possible harm by pornography is by providing sufficient sex information of high calibre at appropriate times in their life cycles to satisfy the natural curiosity which may lead them to pornography."

Many of us never received that kind of training when we grew up, and our curiosity remains. It would be at least honest, if not healthy, to simply admit that we all "enjoy a glimpse of nipple now and then" as readily as we admit to a vicarious thrill "every time Charles Bronson pulls the trigger and a mugger falls dead."

Then, instead of chasing sexual shadows either for comfort or from outrage, we might have a little more time for investing our culture with substance, supporting those positive principles that lead to its healthy growth. When all is said and done, "The Rolls Royce of Hardcore" will turn out to be an Edsel. And any way you look at it, there are more important things to get excited about.

REEL THREE

Violence in the Movies

"Out here, due process is a bullet."
—JOHN WAYNE, in *The Green Berets*

The sticky floor of the movie house smells like stale urine. This once plush Times Square theater threw out the Oriental carpet years ago. You lean back in a seat that threatens to crack like the jaws that crack on the screen. Oriental jaws. You're watching *The Deadly China Doll.*

Five foot three, eyes the color of tea, the Deadly China Doll leaps high in slow motion and kicks her feet into the face of a thug. Slowly he falls, like timber. Dressed in blue pj's that balloon in the breeze, she leaps again. The camera catches her feet as they stomp down on the villain's chest. You watch her grind her feet into his heart, hear the rip of skin, the crunch of bone, and can almost smell the bile spill out of his mouth.

A red school bus chugs up and a battalion of bad guys pour out of windows and doors like soldiers from a toy box. They grunt, yell, and screech. China Doll, as fragile as a bull, positions herself as they circle her for the kill. Kick! Crack! Slap! Pow! Legs snap. Bones break. It's a cartoon. Tom and Jerry in Hong Kong.

A few teen-agers sit with their legs hung over the seats in front of them and yuk it up. A few adult males simply stare.

A solitary bum snores. There are no women in the seamy theater.

China Doll wipes out the whole battalion in three minutes. The day is saved. But you can't remember for what.

Sitting in the warm train on the way home, you watch raindrops slide down the black window like tears, then you pick up the New York *Post*. Another kidnapping. More graft. And the crime rate rises again, four times as fast as the population. But you find it hard to believe that comic-strip fantasies like *The Deadly China Doll* can possibly have anything to do with it. When you were a kid, you and your pals lived on a literary diet of gruesome comic books like *The Vault of Horror, The Crypt of Terror,* and *The Haunt of Fear.* You remember one story about a baseball player who couldn't make the team. Furious, he kills all his teammates and cuts them up into little pieces. He becomes the team. He uses a heart for home plate, intestines for base lines, torsos for bases, a head for the ball, and limbs for bats. How ghoulish can you get? Concerned parents saw that those comics were off the stands by the time you were twelve. But surely it was too late, as you had already digested hundreds of them and the effect was certainly irreversible. So why is it that today some of your pals are doves, others are hawks, and most of you flutter somewhere in between?

Nevertheless, you do suspect that violent movies are more harmful to young people, if not to adults as well, than movies about sex. After all, even when misrepresented, sex is at least fundamentally natural and potentially affirmative, whereas violence is basically unnatural and tends to negate all that is warm and loving in human life. At least that's your point of view. But can the catsupy camp humor of a *Deadly China Doll* have a bad effect on young people? Some experts say yes. Others say no. All have statistics to prove their point of view.

An hour later, you pull your green Opel up the driveway.

A light glows in the living room. Your house looks as warm and inviting as a pumpkin on Halloween. You open the door. Two miniature Minnesota Vikings tackle you around the legs. You lift up each of your small sons and throw them in turn high in the air. "Do it again!" they yell. "Do it again!" You do it one more time, rub your back, then hug your wife who hugs you back. The kids like to see Mommy and Daddy hugging each other. And Mommy and Daddy like to do it. "Sorry I'm late," you say. "But I had to catch a chop-suey Western."

"Was it awful?"

"Not so bad. Just silly. What are you guys up to?"

"Watching cowboys," your older son says. "It's good too. It's about these kids. And they shoot guns." Both sons, dressed in blue pj's with Dumbo the Elephant flying across their chests, sit back on the sofa and stare at the television screen. You slip off your raincoat, throw it over the rocker, and plop down between them. Your wonderful wife hands you a cold glass of Coke with lots of chipped ice. "Thank you, sweetheart."

"You can eat now or later. It makes no difference. The boys are going to bed as soon as this is over."

"I'll just sit with them for a while, O.K.?"

Someone has been playing with the color dials on the television set. The grass is blue, the sky is green, and John Wayne's face is pink. It doesn't take you long to figure out the plot though. The Duke has hired eleven boys who look like innocent acolytes to help him herd his cattle across the range. This must be *The Cowboys*. It played at Radio City Music Hall hardly a year ago, billed as the greatest family movie since *The Sound of Music*. You vaguely recall one reviewer saying that the plot was about how *The Cowboys* trade in their pimples for pistols and learn how to become men by learning how to kill. You wonder if your kids should be watching this, but it is supposed to be a family movie, so you decide to see what happens next.

One boy in the movie has a stuttering problem. Duke, a father figure to all the boys, tells him he'd better stop right now. "I . . . c-c-c-can't," the boy stutters.

"You can if you want to," the Duke intimidates him, getting fiercer with each taunt. Finally the boy spits out an expletive deleted and is cured.

"It's a hard life," Father Duke tells his boys, as if it's a Gospel verse, and seems to imply that there is little room in a man's world for tenderness. At least don't ever show it. During a commercial, you share your Coke with your sons and horse around.

After a commercial that catches your eye in which a lovely girl says, "Do it. There's no excuse not to anymore," you find the cowboys and their father back out in the prairie where they meet up with a madame and her girls. What's this? Not a sex-initiation scene. It doesn't quite come off, though it's suggested that it could, and the movie simply drags on. Your little one puts his head against your shoulder and starts to doze. The real initiation is not into sex but into death, and that begins to take place now. Wayne teaches his sons that there are good guys and bad guys in the world, that things are either black or white, and that there is nothing in between. You remember Marlon Brando's philosophy of life as Terry Malloy in *On the Waterfront:* "Get him before he gets you." But Terry was a pathetic pug in a movie made for adults; Wayne is a gruff godhead in a movie made for families. And it's not a two-bit cartoon like *The Deadly China Doll,* but a five-million-dollar fantasy that looks real.

Surprisingly, Wayne gets knocked off by a vicious rustler, the first time he's bit the dust since he hit *The Sands of Iwo Jima* in 1950. But his children have learned their lessons well. Out in the prairie, due process is a bullet. Justice means revenge. Get him before he gets you. Your little one wakes up. Both boys sense excitement and hunch forward on the sofa. In the movie, the china blue eyes of the children turn to cobalt steel. Together, like a pack of trained marines, they wipe out the whole gang of rustlers. Your children sit on the edge of the sofa. Duke's kids find the monster who killed their father. He is tangled beneath his horse. He begs for mercy. One boy, a glimmer like the reflection of a bayonet in his eyes, fires a rifle into the air. The horse takes off, dragging the man over brambles and briars, stones and weeds, as he bleeds, screams, and writhes in a drawn-out dance of death.

Your older son whispers, "Yaaaay."

"Good," squeaks your little one.

The network obviously cut much of the explicit bloodshed to make this family film even more palatable television fare. But how could they ever cut the point of view? If you have a problem, solve it by force. Might makes right. And the armed will inherit the earth. In *The Cowboys*, unlike in *The Deadly China Doll*, violence goes hand in hand with macho moralisms, masquerading as unequivocal truth. The difference between the two movies is the difference between a comic book and *Mein Kampf*. And *The Cowboys*, unlike *Deep Throat*, is not rated out-of-bounds for your kids.

You get up and switch the set off. "It's time for bed, guys."

But the guys are racing around the living room, yelling "Bang! Bang!" and taking turns at falling dead. The little one grabs a water pistol off a bookshelf and aims it at his older brother. The bigger child takes it away and shoves his brother down. "Mine," cries the little one, "my gun." Both boys are screaming. You separate them. Your wife rushes in.

"Now stop hollering," you holler. "Sit down." Obediently, they sit on top of the sofa, their chins resting on top of their blue bunny pj's, their saucer eyes looking up in anticipation.

You know you can only mouth what might be a platitude too, but you tell them as softly and as sincerely as you can, "Life can be nice, boys. If you want it to be."

Their mother kneels in front of them and squeezes their hands. "Love each other, boys," she says. "Like Mommy and Daddy love you. Okay?"

They smile. It wasn't so bad. And they nod their heads yes. Then kiss each other on the cheek. They do understand.

"Now it's time for bed," their mother says gently but firmly.

Together, you and your wife take them into the bathroom for a last go at the toilet before the long night. Your wife takes the older one into his bedroom, tucks him in, and strokes his head. You take the little one to his bed, sing him a little song about three blind mice, and soon he turns his head and says, "You can go now, Dad."

As you tiptoe toward the door, he raises his head and says, "Dad?"

"Yes, Son?"

"Can I have a gun too?"

The first celluloid cowboy fired his gun in the *Cripple Creek Barroom* in 1898—a movie shot in a converted airplane hangar in East Orange, New Jersey. But I don't believe he was the great-grandfather of *The Cowboys*.

The early Westerns were romantic fantasies and about as lethal as lullabies. In 1914, William S. Hart created a good bad guy (or bad good guy, depending on your point of view) who always redeemed himself in the end through the snow-white love of a schoolmarm. In 1920, Tom Mix began a love affair with his horse. In movies like *Just Tony,* Mix treated audiences to a fancy mix of trick riding and quick drawing. *The Covered Wagon* led the way in 1923 for a wagon train of Westerns that would look back on the golden West not in anger but with loving nostalgia. When sound came to the movies, director King Vidor made a violent mistake. He had Johnny Mack Brown as *Billy the Kid* and Wallace Beery as Pat Garrett make noise with their guns and fists and coated the screen with a veneer of violence that audiences didn't want in their Westerns. The movie was a flop.

I don't think *The Cowboys* evolved so much from the Western as it did from an increasingly violent society and the growing ability of the media to capture that violence in a variety of different ways.

The sexually explicit movies of the '60s, if you think about it, did not precede but accompanied (and were usually a step behind) a sexual revolution that was already taking place in reality. The pill, the feminist movement, the Playboy philosophy, trial marriages, and alternate life-styles, etc., were widespread well before movies began to reflect and perhaps reinforce them. And just as Fatima danced for real in Chicago before Dolorita shimmied on celluloid in Jersey, a similar parallel can be seen in the history of violence in the movies.

When Al Capone's gang wiped out nine rivals on St. Valentine's Day, 1927, it was inevitable that by Christmas a silent movie called *Underworld* would hit the screen with a bang. Written by Ben Hecht, it was the first popular movie to glamorize violence, triggering off a genre that has often changed clothes but never died.

In 1930, Edward G. Robinson starred in one of the first talking mob movies, see, and, as *Little Caesar,* croaked at the end, "Mother of Mercy, is this the end of Rico?"

No way, see.

Rico rose from the grave in 1931 to become Tom Powers, *The Public Enemy.* Played by Jimmy Cagney, today's male chauvinists fondly remember him for pushing a grapefruit into his moll's face because she's getting too pushy, but what thrilled audiences in those days, depressed by the Great Depression, was its Horatio Alger plot of a boy from the bottom who climbs to the top with the aid of a new American invention—the machine gun. Film critic Lewis Jacobs wrote: "The audience saw the tough fighting world where the question of right is thrust aside for the question of might—that world of naked crude essentials by which they themselves were threatened."

In 1932, Tom Powers became Tony Comante in *Scarface,* billed as "the gangster movie to end all gangster movies," and in a way it almost was. Paul Muni was such an attractive carbon of Al Capone that the Legion of Decency, the American Legion, and legions of women's societies and businessmen's clubs protested to their local theaters, Hollywood, and Washington, D.C.

To avoid censorship, Hollywood policed itself. The 1934 production code tamed sex, as you know, but did you know that it also branded brutality an obscenity too?

The code not only forced Mae West to raise her blouse, Betty Boop to lower her skirt, and Gable and Colbert to hang a blanket between them when *It Happened One Night,* but it also insisted that movies no longer glorify violence, nor show "the wholesale slaughter of human beings" as well as any scene that would "tend to lessen the sacredness of human life."

Not only were obscene words like "broad" and "damn" and "S.O.B." banned, but words like "nigger" and "chink" and "kike" as well. "No picture shall be introduced that tends to incite bigotry or hatred among people of differing races, religions or national origins."

Howard Moody was thirteen years old.

Hollywood solved the tension (that now exists on television) between giving people what they want and offering them what they might need by giving them what they would pay for in a different set of clothes.

"PUBLIC ENEMY Becomes Soldier of the Law," boasted the ads for *G Men* in 1935. "Hollywood's Most Famous Bad Man Joins the *G Men* and Halts the March of Crime. . . . The fact that Jimmy Cagney, the historic *Public Enemy* of 1931, now plays the lead in this epic of the end of gangdom, makes its appeal inevitable!" The gang was different but the guns were the same. In reality, cops were chasing robbers all over America, so violence simply put on a badge in movies like *I Am the Law, Racket Busters,* and *Bullets or Ballots.*

By the end of the decade, both the Depression and the violence that came with it were cooling off, and *Little Caesar* went so far as to become *Brother Orchid* and prayed away crime from a monastery. In 1939, Jimmy Cagney took a last look at *The Roaring Twenties* and seemed to kiss the gangster genre good-by. Humphrey Bogart bumps him off, and, in front of a cathedral as Cagney falls down the sanctified steps to his death, his moll eulogizes, "He used to be a big shot."

Meanwhile, across the ocean, gangsters in hobnailed boots marched across the Polish frontier and gave Hollywood a patriotic reason to cross the frontier of violence it had marked for itself. "The wholesale slaughter of human beings" was now a reality. All bets were off. Cagney joined the Canadian Royal Air Force to become *Captain of the Clouds,* Bogie joined the Navy for *Action in the North Atlantic,* and other crooks or cops traded in their fedoras or badges for helmets and stars. Violence splashed across the screen as it spread for real across the world.

On December 7, 1941, Japanese airplanes strafed Pearl Harbor in an obscene attack at dawn. The following February, American soldiers rounded up 110,000 Japanese-American citizens and herded them into detention camps on the West Coast for being Japanese. A few months later, John Garfield played an angry gunner in *Air Force* who cries out, "We're getting kicked all over the place by a lot of stinking Nips!" He rips apart a Zero. We watch the Japanese pilot pitch forward with a sliver of blood running down his chin. Another gunner shouts, "Fried Jap going down!" At the end, Garfield's plane leads a raid over Tokyo. And the pilot exults, "We're going to play 'The Star-spangled Banner' with two-ton bombs!"

But it wasn't John Garfield who exclaimed: "We shall wipe them out, every one of them, men, women and children. There shall not be a Japanese left on the face of the earth." It was Winston Churchill. The movies of the '40s reflected and reinforced the specific feelings of a specific culture in a time of war.

And there were scores of them.

As well as hundreds of newsreels and documentaries, often vivid anthologies of atrocities committed by the Germans and Japanese. Such films not only whetted our appetite for vengeance but perhaps increased our threshold for visual violence as well. "When you make such a picture," James Agee wrote in 1945, "or watch it with untroubled approval, some crucially important nerve has, I believe, gone dead in you." Surely, anything that followed would have to be an anticlimax.

By the late '40s, when kids like me weren't running to a Saturday matinee to cheer John Wayne in *The Sands of Iwo Jima* or to hiss James Mason as *The Desert Fox,* we were jumping and screaming through fifteen cartoons, yelling "yaaaaaaaaaaay" as the first one started, not stopping until it was over, and beginning again for fourteen more. Poet John Houseman wrote at the time: "Today the animated cartoon has become a bloody battlefield through which savage and remorseless creatures with single-track minds, pursue one another, then rend, gouge, twist, tear and mutilate each other with sadistic ferocity." When we weren't watching movies or cartoons, we were either trading our *Crypt of Terror*s for *Vault of Horror*s or playing soldiers in empty lots and prairies.

Living in that time was like walking around in a black-and-white movie without a happy ending. Even the melodramas had the bitter taste of ashes left in the mouth, after "winning" a war in which there are no real winners at all. Exactly ten years after *The Roaring Twenties*, Jimmy Cagney came back as a gangster with an Oedipus complex in *White Heat*. He climbs to the top of a chemical tower, cries out, "Made it, Ma! Top of the world!" and blows himself to pieces along with everything else.

"It's what people want me to do," Jimmy lamented. "Someday though, I'd like to make just one picture kids could go see."

In 1950, television aerials began to sprout on American rooftops like flowers from outer space. Kids at home now watched Hopalong Cassidy, Roy Rogers, and Gene Autry sing, ride, and draw just as kids in the '20s watched Tom Mix, William S. Hart, and Buck Jones at the movies. If movies are always a step behind reality, early television was decades behind it. But movie attendance sank to sixty million from its ninety million peak in 1948. The new invention was changing the habits of Americans. And movies had to change with it.

Even Westerns.

To attract a new audience, filmmakers crossed the frontier of fantasy and entered the land of Freud. The sad hero of *White Heat* put on a holster. And Gregory Peck as *The*

Gunfighter became symbolic of a new kind of gunslinger more victimized by violence than the victims he is forced to kill. The adult Western was born. *Broken Arrow* featured Jeff Chandler as a Jewish Cochise in the first movie to paint Indians white, or good, since the silent days.

As well as guilt, fascination with weaponry followed the war, and Westerns glorified the tools of death used in the nineteenth century—the *Winchester 73* and the *Colt 45,* the cannon in the *Battle of Apache Pass,* the Gatling gun in *The Siege of Red River,* and an eight-inch Bowie knife in *The Iron Mistress,* movies made between 1950 and 1954.

By 1954, many of those children whose fathers had dodged bullets during the '40s or whose brothers were sharpening bayonets in Korea began to form gangs with guns and knives that shocked the nation. A Senate subcommittee studied the causes of juvenile delinquency. And the subject was explored in movies like *The Blackboard Jungle, Rebel Without a Cause,* and *The Wild One.*

The brutal inhabitants of *The Blackboard Jungle* make the Dead End Kids look like choirboys, and the cause of delinquency is laid on poverty and race. In *Rebel Without a Cause,* the delinquents come from middle-class suburban homes. As James Dean's parents only scratch the surface of his problem, he screams in anguish, "You're tearing me apart!" and forms a gang with Natalie Wood and Sal Mineo that is more like a family than his own. In *The Wild One,* Marlon Brando gives a classic imitation of Marlon Brando, and the blame seems to fall at the wheels of a Harley-Davidson. A French review entitled "The Martians Have Landed" describes *The Wild One* as "a film without explanations, judgments or justifications. An absurd, brutal awkward film; an abstruse, fascinating, animalistic Marlon Brando who searches out and provokes distress, disquiet, and discomfort because, I imagine, Benedek (the director) and the authors find the world disquieting and uncomfortable."

While juveniles were getting into violence following two back-to-back wars, organized crime was back in business too, and the Senate investigated the mobs as well. Movies reflected the bad new days by recreating the good old days in the mood of the '50s with *Murder, Inc., The Purple Gang,* and *The Rise and Fall of Legs Diamond.* Mickey Rooney said good-by to Andy Hardy and became a wrinkled *Baby Face Nelson.* Charles Bronson got his first death wish as *Machine Gun Kelly.* And Rod Steiger as *Al Capone* mumbled the new theme: "I'm not a gangster. I'm a businessman. Serve the public. That's my motto." On the home screen, *The Untouchables* was the viewer's choice, and local stations ran old-time movies like *Little Caesar* and *The Public Enemy,* no longer out-of-bounds, but curiosity pieces on a twelve-inch screen.

And, as the '50s came to a close, an older Jimmy Cagney made *Mister Roberts, The Seven Little Foys,* and *Man of a Thousand Faces*—three funny, delightful, and tender movies that kids everywhere could and did enjoy.

The '50s didn't really end until 1963.

Lee Harvey Oswald fired two long bullets through President John F. Kennedy's head on November 22. Almost every one of us watched it on television. And watched it again and again. And watched Jack Ruby split open Oswald's guts with a handgun. Again and again. Television became reality. We saw that murder is messy and that death carries pain to those who survive. It was a nationwide exercise both in mourning and in voyeurism. From that moment on, slowly but surely, the movies added a new element to screen violence. It was no longer enough for a character to be shot and fall down dead like kids playing soldiers in an empty lot. Now we had to see the blood, the bits of brain, the pain, the agony, the flies on the corpse.

The new frontier was passed quietly at first in grind houses now losing money on the last small wave of nudies. Before the next sexual step beyond, the grind houses took in profits from a genre of hideous movies known as the "ghoulies." In 1963, a producer named David Friedman, who proudly refers to himself as "the Hitchcock of the crotch operas," made a little movie called *Blood Feast.* Violence for the sake of violence, his little feast cost the usual $25,000, took in $1,200,000, and gave birth to other ghoulies like *I Eat Your Flesh* and *I Drink Your Blood.* Theater managers passed out vomit bags to customers. These movies featured torture, whippings, crucifixions, and dismembering with knives, hatchets, and saws. A handful of them got into trouble with local censors, but most of the cutting took place on the screen. "Paradoxically," write Turan and Zito, "these grotesque films, featuring neither complete nudity nor loving sexual contact, were largely exempt from the wrath of the censors, possibly because the United States has traditionally been a country that censors sex but tolerates violence."

So the question asked by movie moguls in Reel Two about explicit sex was raised again about explicit violence: "If brutality can be shown in shlock movies and make money, why not put it into high-class products too?"

During the next four years, bullets slowly ground deeper into bellies, knives drew more and more drops of blood, but only a few people noticed the gradual change. In the 1966 *The Chase,* Sheriff Marlon Brando's face is pounded into a saucy pizza by angry townspeople who are furious because he will not give them Robert Redford. But in 1966, Brando was on the way down, Redford was hardly on the way up, and not many people saw the movie. It wasn't until 1967—the same year that Watts, Detroit, and Newark erupted in flames—that a popular movie would blaze across the explicit frontier, stirring the senses and causing controversy.

"They're young!" screamed the ads. "They're in love! And they kill people!"

Bullets in the face. Blood soaking through clothes. And a slow-motion dance of death. It was in the open. It was new. And it broke the bank.

Bonnie and Clyde, directed by Arthur Penn, who also did *The Chase,* was enjoying its biggest success in 1968 when Sirhan Sirhan put a bullet in Senator Robert Kennedy's head. Life magazine expressed a growing public sentiment: "The shooting of Robert Kennedy increases the concern and the debate over the possible effects of the climate of violence that pervades today's world, where real life and fictional— as in the popular movie *Bonnie and Clyde*—are filled with images of brutality." Meanwhile, each night Americans were treated by television to images of torture and killing in a real country called Vietnam.

Arthur Schlesinger put together a paperback on "the pornography of violence," and attacked *Bonnie and Clyde* for "its blithe acceptance which almost became a celebration." Meanwhile, the Weathermen had long since planted their last bomb in a New York building, Martin Luther King was predicting his own death, Parisian students were trashing the Champs-Élysées, Russian tanks were rumbling into Czechoslovakia, cops were cracking young skulls at the Democratic Convention in Chicago, and blood continued to turn the rice paddies red in Vietnam.

A pretty big burden to place on the shoulders of two shadows called *Bonnie and Clyde.*

But the situation was similar to the 1931 uproar over *The Public Enemy,* and *Bonnie and Clyde* soon changed their '30s clothes for cowboy outfits. Sam Peckinpah's *The Wild Bunch* gave us a macho look at the Old West at the turn of the century, featuring so many slow-motion ballets of death that the technique became a cliché before the movie was over. Critics of the film tried to count the dead bodies in the movie but could not. The only body count available that year was the one delivered by Walter Cronkite on the evening news: "The Pentagon reports today that seven of our fighting men have died in Vietnam. Seventeen South Vietnamese are reported dead. And 456 of the enemy."

In 1968, another movie phenomenon was overtaking America—the Clint Eastwood craze. It started with *A Fistful of Dollars,* made with a fistful of lire by Sergio Leone in 1967. The first of the "spaghetti Westerns," it went on to make both Leone and Eastwood millionaires. Critic Judith Crist was one of many outraged by its casual attitude toward "men and women [being] gouged, burned, beaten, stomped, and shredded to death." Curiously, *A Fistful of Dollars* was not only made by an Italian but he got his idea from a Japanese movie directed by Akira Kurosawa called *Yojimbo,* which was even bloodier. What was unique, perhaps, about the cowboy version was not so much its explicit brutality but its indifferent attitude toward life itself as being of any value and that it caught on in America while the humanistic Japanese movie played only in art houses.

The Eastwood character—The Man With No Name— soon appeared in another movie, *For a Few Dollars More* (which it made), and in *The Good, the Bad, and the Ugly* (which it was). Richard Harmet in the Los Angeles *Free Press* tried to explain the craze: "There seemed about him the absolute certainty that he stood above the rest of mankind, and that there was no one he couldn't take with his gun or his fists. Unconcerned about a higher moral order, he shot those who stood in his way." Ironically, the Man With No Name never seemed much interested in sex.

Everyone hoped that the '70s would be nicer than the '60s. They weren't. President Nixon, after declaring that the war that was going on in Vietnam was over, declared a war against crime at home. And, oddly enough, as *The Public Enemy* had become one of the *G Men* in 1935, the Man With No Name became a new kind of American cop—*Dirty Harry.* Dirty Harry is a brutal bigot who goes outside the law to catch and kill a brutal maniac. Director Don Siegel proudly calls it "a wall to wall carpet of violence." Pauline Kael of *The New Yorker* calls it "fascist." In two years, *Dirty Harry* outgrosses *Snow White* and *Pinocchio* combined. And gives birth to a mob of movie cops who make *Little Caesar* look like *Little Lord Fauntleroy.*

In the mid-'70s, it's no longer possible to tell the good guys from the bad guys. Presumably, we're supposed to root for whomever manages to survive. As for the frontier movies of the recent past, like *The Wild One, Bonnie and Clyde,* and *The Wild Bunch,* you can catch them on television when you're not watching *Mannix* or *Kojak* or *Cannon.* The 1927 *Underworld* comes full circle in the 1975 *Godfather II,* when Al Pacino as Michael Corleone sums up fifty years of movies and life: "If history has taught us anything, it is that you can kill anyone."

Now for some not so instant analysis.

I'll bet my son's water pistol that I caught almost every World War II movie as a child. They made me feel proud. After all, my father was fighting a war I didn't understand in a country I never even heard of, and the heroes of movies like *I Wanted Wings* made me imagine him. A particular thrill for me was the 1949 *Command Decision* in which my father actually appeared. Remember how those war movies would splice in actual documentary footage to add realism to the plot? In that film, a real group of fly-boys jump off of a truck and run to their planes for an important mission. One of them was clearly my dad. I saw the movie three times.

And I'll bet that Jane Fonda, who is about my age, saw most of those movies too and was as moved as we were all supposed to be at the time.

But if we can point to a pornography of piety as well as to a pornography of sex, it is even easier to apply the principles behind the blue door to a pornography of propaganda. Especially one coated with violence. And this isn't just Monday morning quarterbacking thirty years after the fact. James Agee, writing for *Fortune* back in 1945, had something to say about a savage documentary that can well be applied to many fictional war films as well:

"Very uneasily, I am beginning to believe that, for all that may be said in favor of our seeing these terrible records of war, we have no business seeing this sort of experience except through our presence and participation. . . . Whatever the effects it may or may not have, pornography is invariably degrading to anyone who looks at or reads it. If at an incurable distance from participation, hopelessly incapable of reactions adequate to the event, we watch men killing each other, we may be quite as profoundly degrading ourselves and, in the process, betraying and separating ourselves the farther from those we are trying to identify ourselves with; none the less because we tell ourselves sincerely that we sit in comfort and watch carnage in order to nurture our patriotism, our conscience, our understanding and our sympathies."

The attack on Pearl Harbor is, of course, a greater obscenity than the subsequent imprisonment of American citizens for having yellow skin and slanted eyes. But that doesn't make the latter any less obscene. Nor the movies like *Air Force* that not only reflect but perhaps reinforce an attitude of racial hatred that lingers still today. If a valid argument against specific sex movies is that they distort reality by taking the part and making it the whole, what do we say about movies that universalize *all* Germans as cold-blooded killers or *all* Japanese as sneering sadists?

The Purple Heart, made in 1943, is not unique in seeming to embody the entire Japanese nation in the particular character created by Richard Loo. If you recall, Loo was often the sly Japanese general who, with a crooked smile on his wicked face, would say something like this to a noble Dana Andrews: "Why, of course I speak English, Major. I studied engineering at your University of California. Now you will sign this confession or I will have my men slowly tear off your fingernails, one by one." I saw *The Purple Heart* on television on a recent Sunday afternoon, and it still has the contrived power to stir the senses. And it made me recall a real-life scene that took place on the playground of an American orphanage hardly five years ago. Several boys were running in and out of the steel jungle of seesaws, swings, and slides, playing a game of soldiers. An older boy taunted a smaller third-generation Japanese-American boy. "Go on, Nip. Fall down the slide. You gotta die. The Nips gotta die." The word "Nip" was not even used as a derogatory expression. It had become the boy's nickname. He fell down the slide and "died."

Existentially, pornography is a frontier phenomenon, encompassing specific material considered out-of-bounds by a specific culture at a specific time. A movie about the obscenity of Issei and Nissei, those first- and second-generation Japanese Americans locked up on the West Coast because of their heritage, would have been out-of-bounds in 1943. I won't be surprised if it's made into an acceptable, if not ignored, movie soon. What surprises me is that movies like *The Purple Heart* are so casually accepted in 1975 as mild entertainment for a Sunday afternoon. As Drs. Marvin Heller and Samuel Polsky observe such movies "may be palatable to large numbers of the viewing audience on patriotic grounds in a country at war. To persevere with such fare in peacetime can only contribute to a dehumanized concept of man." I'm not at all suggesting their disappearance; I'm just trying to understand why movies like *Deep Throat* are considered a menace while movies like *The Purple Heart* are considered inspiring.

The pornography of violent propaganda is as one-dimensional as any other pornography, if that's how one chooses to describe the term. During World War II, Hollywood no longer glorified the machine gun but glamorized new lethal inventions like *Dive Bombers, Flying Tigers,* submarines in *Destination Tokyo,* and PT boats in *They Were Expendable* (the boats were not expendable, but the men who rode in them were). The general effect was to make war look clean, easy, even romantic. If *Deep Throat* is a sexual mirage, then *Dive Bombers* is a military mirage. And which of these is more obscene, if either of them, depends on your point of view. But the principle applies to both.

The British applied the principle to *Objective Burma* in 1945. It was an exciting movie about a key battle, and they resented the fact that Errol Flynn captures the front without any suggestion of the British blood that had been paving the way for a year. The effect of this and many other American films is to give the impression that we won World War II all by ourselves. Many of us, I'm sure, still believe it. And one wonders if the British have forgiven us yet.

However, if some movies exploited the violence of war for either patriotic or commercial reasons or both, others explored it with depth and understanding. I'll always remember William Wellman's wonderful *Story of G.I. Joe* with Burgess Meredith as journalist Ernie Pyle. A quiet movie, it accuses no one and offers no solutions but, simply by being true to its own vision, stands as one of the clearest and loudest statements against violence ever made.

Major John Huston, who as a civilian made the classic

Maltese Falcon in 1941, shot several documentaries for the Army that are forgotten works of art. His *Let There Be Light* didn't see the light for years. It is an honest documentary about combat neurosis—how war can shatter even the survivors—and about the humanitarian efforts of doctors and nurses to treat the victims. "No scenes were staged," runs the opening credit. "The cameras merely recorded what took place in an Army hospital." Huston called it "the most hopeful and optimistic and even joyous thing I had a hand in. I felt as though I were going to church every day out in that hospital." It is hardly a movie to encourage new recruits, and Washington buried it in a sanctuary of the War Department..

The Story of G.I. Joe and *Let There Be Light* were neither prowar nor antiwar films, though by showing the effects of violence, spiritual as well as physical, they did have pacifist implications. Equally important in this regard were two movies made after the war, *The Best Years of Our Lives* in 1946 and *The Men* in 1950. These four movies, however, are like diamonds in a field of land mines.

I can't help suspecting that the great battalion of movies that glamorized World War II also form a landmark in the evolution of violent movies to come. Whatever its motives, Hollywood crossed its own frontier in 1940 and treated moviegoers to "the wholesale slaughter of human beings" in a socially acceptable way. To be sure, violent movies accompanied World War I too, but the cinema was in its infancy then, and they were few. And the handful of war movies that followed, like *All Quiet on the Western Front* and *What Price Glory?* are notable for their nonviolent themes. World War II, more than World War I, was a "popular" war, and at that time Hollywood was a major industry. For ten years, it bombarded our eyes and minds with literally hundreds of movies and newsreels and documentaries whose cumulative effect would surely "tend to lessen the sacredness of human life." The only frontier left to cross was to revel in the blood. What surprises me is that it took twenty years.

War is certainly a far greater obscenity than the movies that glorify it, but that doesn't make the latter any less obscene. At the same time, if movies like *The Purple Heart* seem more obscene than movies like *Dirty Harry,* that doesn't make the latter any less obscene either. In fact, they may be more so or not at all so, depending on your point of view. Again, as with sex in the movies, the dilemma is not only to distinguish the exploitation of violence from its honest exploration but, more importantly, to try to determine if today's rash of violent movies is simply symptomatic of a violent society or is, in fact, contributing to the disease.

Violence has been a key dramatic theme from Aeschylus through Shakespeare to Arrabal. To insist that it not be treated at all would be one-dimensional, distorted, and a mirage.

But when it comes to specific movies, it's not always easy to separate the wheat from the chaff. Sometimes they seem to grow together in the same film.

Walking Tall is a violent movie about violence whose visual thrills are secondary to a story that could stand on its own. It has a strong moral vision, whether you agree with its particular metaphysics or not, beneath and supported by its graphic montage. So you try to accept it on its own artistic terms and evaluate it as you would any other movie about another human experience. But you still feel uneasy.

Even though the movie shows the aftermath of violence— grief, separation, loss—you can't help questioning what seems to be a lurid lingering on explicit scenes of brutality. You wonder if showing a knife slowly slicing the hero's chest is really essential to carve out the movie's theme, and you think of movies like *The Hustler* in which two thugs break Paul Newman's knuckles behind a closed toilet stall. In that movie, you don't see a thing. You hear something. You imagine everything. And the effect is more dramatic than a clinical close-up.

So how do you evaluate *Walking Tall*? All you know is that it packs a wallop, that millions of people love it, that you feel both uplifted and let down, and that its director Phil Karlson is not a charlatan. So you give everyone the benefit of your own personal doubt and, with an ambivalent feeling you can't quite define, walk small to another movie.

The Astor Plaza is a modern theater buried in the bowels of a glass and steel skyscraper in mid-Manhattan. You descend the escalator like a contemporary Don Quixote on the way to a tasteful dungeon. A Coney Island of a candy counter looms large on the edge of a carpet that spreads into infinity like an acrylon beach. You enter a vast auditorium with enough seats to accomodate the population of Poughkeepsie. Several hundred people sit scattered in the tiered rows that stretch from the screen to the projection booth a block away. Everyone is here to make a *Death Wish*.

You know the story by heart. Who doesn't? But you've idolized Charles Bronson ever since he dug that tunnel all by himself in *The Great Escape*. What a man.

The movie begins. Bronson and wife, Hope Lange, who wears a stunning bathing suit, are sunning themselves in Hawaii. What a body.

Not Hope's. Chuck's. The man is over fifty, old enough to be your father, but it's clear from the start that he can knock you flat with a flick of his Fu Manchu moustache.

Chuck and Hope return home to New York. Right away you suspect exploitation. Their cab is stuck in a noisy traffic jam on the Queensboro Bridge. The idea is to show the crowded urban conditions that lead to crime. But any New Yorker knows that to get from Kennedy Airport to Manhattan you don't take the Queensboro Bridge but the Triboro or the Midtown Tunnel. Bronson is being exploited by his cabby and ought to knock him flat.

Half a day later, they make it home. They live in a spacious apartment on the West Side, not far from where Rosemary had her baby. They kiss their daughter who is not a baby but a lovely young thing. Everyone in the movie is a thing.

The next day you discover that Bronson is a brilliant architect. You already know that he can dig tunnels with his bare hands. You find it hard to accept that the same person can design urban malls. You wonder if maybe Paul Newman should be playing this part.

While Chuck is at the drawing board, his wife and daughter are at the supermarket. Three young hoods jump out from behind the frozen turkeys and hop up and down like chickens with their heads cut off. You get the point: they're not human. The animals follow the women home and, in a rape scene directed with all the subtlety of a five-car collision, stomp Hope to death and turn her daughter into a zombie.

You do get to see the husband grieve, but it doesn't sit too well because it's tough for Chuck the actor to even fake a tear. You wonder if maybe Brando should have this part.

To get away from it all, Chuck takes an assignment out West where he designs a model village for a wealthy cowboy. To give Chuck a break from his work, the cowboy takes him to a shooting range. Chuck refuses to handle the gun. He confesses that he was a pacifist during the war. And you thought he was digging tunnels. Coaxed into it, Chuck hits the bull's-eye every time. He also confesses that he was raised on a farm. Gary Cooper would have been ideal.

When Chuck gets back home to New York, he discovers that the cowboy has slipped a Colt 45 into his suitcase as a gift. Before too long, still sorrowing over his loss and goaded beyond belief by an environment that seems more like Dodge City than Fun City, Chuck not only shoots muggers but sets them up for the kill.

And many people in the audience do cheer and clap. But you can't help wondering if they're cheering because they're supposed to—isn't that what the ads say everybody does?—or because the scenes are so well done that they elicit a spontaneous response. From your point of view, they are as packed with tension as the Kodak mural in Grand Central Station.

At least the director believes in equal opportunity. Whites, blacks, and Puerto Ricans get to mug and be plugged by Bronson in equal measure. You've already seen his grief, but you never get a glimpse of the sorrow of the families of the muggers. One of them looks like a ten-year-old boy. But they're all animals, so what the hell.

The "vigilante" becomes a national hero. His good example inspires others to take the law into their own hands. New York's crime rate drops dramatically. But New York's finest don't think ordinary citizens should play *Dirty Harry,* so when Bronson finally gets caught, they quietly ship him off to Chicago.

At Union Station, Chuck bends over to pick up a fallen briefcase. He spots three young toughs harassing a young girl. He cocks his fingers into a gun. Aims at the hoods. And smiles. Freeze.

The audience cheers. They can expect a *Death Wish II.*

It is a typical Michael Winner film. Winner, a director with a pedestrian flair for exploiting both violence and Bronson in movies like *The Mechanic* and *The Stone Killer,* uses the same formula in *Death Wish,* but because it exploits urban fears and offers urban moviegoers a savior for an hour and a half of vicarious vengeance, Winner has his first real winner.

But as you leave the underground palace, you study the faces of your fellow death wishers, and they don't look exploited at all. They look pleased. Perhaps the movie does have a cathartic effect. One thing is certain: nobody will be so foolish as to go out and do likewise. Normal mortals know they're not Charles Bronson. The movie would have worked better if—now you've got it—Dustin Hoffman had played the part. Now there's someone you can identify with. Of course, Dusty would have been knocked flat by his cabby and the movie would have never gotten off the ground.

Sure, *Death Wish* is junk. But so is *Deep Throat*. And so are most movies. Why all the controversy? And why this ambivalent feeling you still can't pin down?

As you leave the dungeon, you breathe in the crisp winter air and walk down Broadway. You notice the neon time that runs around the Allied Chemical Tower in a great big hurry. You still have time for one more movie. You catch the nearest one. *The Deadly China Doll.* And that night, after watching a cowboy movie on television with your two small sons, a two-year-old child straightens your ambivalence out.

What is troubling is not any specific movie, and certainly not the portrayal of violence per se, but its growing dominance in movies of every kind, both at the show and at home. Sexual films are a drop in the bucket compared to the flood of blood that fills the screens. For every *Deep Throat* there are a dozen *Death Wishes.* For every middle-aged man who sees a "loop," several million young people see a *Deadly China Doll.* For every adult who goes to a *Last Tango,* tens of millions of men, women, and children stand in line for a *Walking Tall.* Movie attendance has dropped from its sixty million low in 1950 to forty million today, but more people have seen *The Godfather* than have seen any other movie in history. And they can see it on television for the rest of the century. We may be in a situation analogous to the early '40s, when movies bombarded our senses with scenes whose cumulative effect was surely to "lessen the sacredness of life." Only now the bombs make bigger holes. And they continue to glamorize the brutality they pretend to deplore.

Pauline Kael, reviewing Stanley Kubrick's controversial *Clockwork Orange,* observes that today "we are gradually being conditioned to accept violence as a sensual pleasure. The directors used to say that they were showing us its real face and how ugly it was in order to sensitize us to its horrors. You don't have to be very keen to see that they are now in fact desensitizing us. They are saying that everyone is brutal, and the heroes must be as brutal as the villains or they turn into fools." Ms. Kael is not advocating censorship but simply is trying to analyze the possible implications of violent films. "Actually," she points out, "those who believe in censorship are primarily concerned with sex, and they generally worry about violence only when it's eroticized. This means that practically no one raises the issue of the possible cumulative effects of movie brutality. Yet surely, when night after night atrocities are served up as entertainment, it's worth some anxiety."

Ironically, experts have been studying the effects of visual violence for more than twenty years, but, until recently, not many of us have been listening.

That same Senate subcommittee that investigated juvenile delinquency in 1954, headed by Estes Kefauver, also studied the effect of televised violence on human behavior. Violence on television, except when it's live or on the news, has always been a pussycat compared to movie violence, so any learnings from television, if valid, apply even more strongly to movies. It's hard to believe but Kefauver's study suggested that television violence, even then, is potentially harmful to young people.

Network executives promised to reform, but later surveys by the subcommittee in 1961 and 1964 revealed that violence in prime time had in fact increased dramatically. Senator Thomas Dodd issued findings that suggested a possible connection between visual violence and antisocial behavior among juveniles.

In 1968—the year of the peak of *Bonnie and Clyde*—President Johnson created another committee to crack another paradox. He asked the National Commission on the Causes and Prevention of Violence to answer the question: "Are the seeds of violence nurtured through the public airways . . . that reach the family and our young?"

Half a year later, the Commission stated that violence on television does encourage real violence in life, especially among the children of the poor, but it also admitted that its findings were inconclusive and recommended further study.

In March 1969, the Surgeon General got into the operation, and, after a brief examination, concluded that if television can malignantly affect human behavior, then it can also have benign effects. "We must learn more about how to promote this latter capability while we learn to avoid the hazards of the former." The number one doctor charged the National Institute of Mental Health with the responsibility of finding out more about both. Surveys, studies, and tests began on a widespread scale.

Later that year, in its fourth report, the National Commission on Violence, after its exhaustive research, issued a definitive statement. Television, with its "constant portrayal of violence," is "pandering to a public preoccupation with violence that television itself has helped to create." Furthermore, "violence on television encourages violent forms of behavior and fosters moral and social values about violence in daily life which are unacceptable in a civilized society." The Commission concluded, not that television violence was

a primary cause of violence in real life but that it is a contributing factor and that it can have particularly adverse
effects upon children.

Some people cheered. Other people hissed. And most people turned on the television.

A year later, the Surgeon General released his report, also
a definitive statement, one that seemed to tone down the
power of the Commission's report considerably. It concluded
that television violence, while it may tend to modify a child's
attitudes toward violence, really has little effect on society at
all and that the increase in violent crimes is attributable to
social and economic conditions.

Those who cheered now hissed. The hissers cheered. And
most people turned on the television.

So again we come full circle.

What do you think?

That's what it comes down to, you know. Your personal
point of view.

Are you a samurai, a nobleman, a wife, or a woodcutter?

Or perhaps a bit of them all.

conclusion

From this woodcutter's point of view, I think it's witch-
hunting to blame violent movies at the theater or on TV for
our violent world, but it's also a death wish to think that they
are part of the cure. And I'm sure that the family is a far
greater factor than the television set in the family room.
What worries me is not the possibility that brutal movies lead
to a violent world but the probability that a violent world
leads to brutal movies whose cumulative effect is to condition
us to accept that violent world as it is.

First of all, movies follow life. They never lead it. In 1927,
The Underworld would never have hit the screen with a bang
at Christmas if there hadn't first been real bullets and real
corpses in a real alley on St. Valentine's Day. There would

have been no *Purple Hearts* at all in the '40s without a real war that started in 1941. There would have been no *Blackboard Jungle* and no *Rebel Without a Cause* if real-life fathers and brothers had not first fought for causes in real jungles thousands of miles away from home. Those movies came after the rise in juvenile delinquency, not before it. And *Bonnie and Clyde,* as we've seen, did not kill John Kennedy, Robert Kennedy, or Martin Luther King or start the Vietnam war. Finally, long before Charles Bronson discovered a Colt 45 in his suitcase, muggers were mugging and peaceful American citizens made up the best armed society in the history of the world. Today, estimates put the number of privately owned arms in the United States at more than a hundred million, an average of one gun for every two citizens. And each day 30 Americans kill 30 other Americans with handguns. Violent movies are only the shadows of a far more violent world. And television, except when it's on the spot of reality, is hardly a shadow of the shadow.

Thomas A. Shine, a concerned citizen speaking to a Senate subcommittee on communications, feels that our Government is not as concerned with stopping violence in reality as it is with censoring its shadows. Movies and television, he feels, "are in their own crude way reflecting the country's lifestyle and civilization. It should come as no surprise that the television screens portray violence when violence has always been and still is the basic American way, our civilization. The United States Government has always spent so much more money on defense and instruments of war, than on education and the arts. The United States Government has always promoted the military image of violence as a sign of manliness, and has always legalized certain forms of violence, especially those used by law enforcement agencies. In movies, books and television, violence has been inspired directly by the lawfully condoned violent lifestyle of America.

I personally find it difficult for any Senator to be aghast at a graphic scene on 'Hawaii 5–0' when the real-life counterpart uses violence that makes 'Hawaii 5–0' seem mild. The government has no problem sanctioning Kent State's bloody trouble, but for some reason worries about far less violent scenes on television."

However, I also agree with Dr. Bertram Brown, of the National Institute of Mental Health, who argues that constant exposure to these shadows can make us less sensitive to the violence that is real, by gradually extinguishing our emotional responses. "Repeated exposure," he says, "builds the feeling that violent behavior is normal and appropriate under certain circumstances."

I'm not so concerned with items like the newspaper headline that asks: "Did Killer of 3 Follow TV Script?" In that story, we learn that police in Los Angeles are studying a possible connection between a segment on the television series *Police Story* and several skid row deaths in which the throat of each victim had been slashed. I suspect that abnormal people would find a way to commit murder from watching *The Waltons* as well as from watching *Police Story*. In fact, that particular segment on *Police Story* was based on a real case that took place long before it was reinterpreted on the screen. What concerns me more is the effect of a steady diet of visual violence on normal people like myself, if you can accept that presupposition.

I turn to the sports page of the *Daily News*. A routine headline catches my eye: "Polis Credits the Fight." And I read with relish about a young hockey player, benched the previous game, who becomes a hero the next night through what has become a "normal and appropriate" way of behavior:

"Polis decided the best remedy for ridding himself of his pent-up frustration was to get into a fight. It happened with

3:12 to play in St. Louis in a 22-minute brawl in which the Rangers and Blues set an NHL record with 246 game penalty minutes and another record with 186 penalty minutes in one period.

" 'It was quite a donneybrook,' said the skating gladiator, laughing. 'The best I've ever been in. When I'm frustrated and things aren't going well, I've always found the best way to try and turn things around is to let loose in a real good brawl.' "

Here is a case of reality and shadow meeting at the same time. Thousands of people watched that game on television and either hissed or booed, depending on their point of view of who was winning the fight. And I'll be the first to admit that if I hadn't submitted to watching *Rhoda* that night, I would have been cheering as loud as anyone else.

The woodcutter looks into the mirror and sees a samurai.

Then he blinks his eyes and asks another question.

But what about the cathartic effect of vicarious violence? Didn't Aristotle suggest that viewing tragedy can drain away our demonic impulses to commit violence or "to let loose in a real good brawl"? But the nobleman in the woodcutter also knows that Aristotle was talking about the Oedipus family, who liked to do their killings offstage. What would he make of the Corleone family's, and all their vicious cousins' killing up front? Do the rules of his *Poetics* still apply? Are today's violent films safety valves, triggers, or perhaps something else entirely?

Konrad Lorenz is not encouraging. "It's a very real question," says the anthropologist, "whether encouraging people to feel a vicarious destructive aggressivity increases the probability of such aggressivity, or whether the vicarious aggression acts as catharsis. . . . If children are accustomed to seeing wars, murders and fights on TV, their inhibitions against committing these violent acts may lessen. It's not that you're increasing the potential for aggressivity, but that you're low-ering the inhibitions by creating a social climate that toler-ates aggressive acts."

Well, that applies to children. What about grown-ups?

Scientist Leonard Berkowitz, after testing adults exposed to a variety of violent stimuli, concludes that "the observa-tion of aggression is more likely to induce hostile behavior than to drain off aggressive inclinations."

Well, that's just science. What about art?

Art critic Lawrence Alloway, in a study of violent movies called *Violent America,* observes: "Our experience of violent movies, viewed in relation to the findings of experimental psychologists, casts doubt on the idea of purging by enter-tainment."

The woodcutter faces the truth.

He has come to *enjoy* watching violence from a distance.

And it has nothing to do with catharsis.

He is not consoled by Edmund Burke, who wrote when there were no movies or television: "This is not an unmixed delight, but blended with no small uneasiness." The wood-cutter's uneasiness grows when he recalls Pauline Kael's suggestion that he is perhaps "gradually being conditioned to accept violence as a sensual pleasure." He knows that he will never go out and deliberately commit a violent act; he is mythic wife as well as nobleman and samurai. But mainly he is a woodcutter, standing behind a tree and, through his eyes and ears, learning to find pleasure in pain.

The woodcutter recalls Howard Moody's definition of ob-scenity. Any material, whether sexual or not, that tends to debase, degrade, or dehumanize persons. And if he now knows nothing else, it is that the pornography of violence fits that definition far better than any pornography of sex.

At least hard-core sex movies, even those without love, arouse a natural impulse and by their very nature suggest the possibility of intimacy with another human being. But violent movies that glamorize brutality seem to sensualize an unnatural impulse and by their very nature suggest the separation of human beings. And yet we have been taught that the natural instinct is a vice and that the unnatural is a virtue. It is time to turn our heads around.

Existentially, pornography is a frontier phenomenon, encompassing specific material considered out-of-bounds by a specific culture at a specific time. And it's beginning to look like violent movies, simply by power of their enormous foothold, are stirring more senses and beginning to cause almost as much controversy as all the movies to cross the sexual frontier.

But violence in movies will not vanish until it begins to diminish in our own lives. Movies mirror who and what we are. They will change as we change. Thomas Shine writes: "The American approach to life, the government attitude of confrontations, power and might through force has to change. Non-violence must be promoted as seriously and actively as the present military image is today. The basic attitude both in action and rhetoric must be one of non-violent solutions to problems. Though this bit of idealism would probably never succeed entirely, or even significantly alter our way of life, it would be a giant step for mankind in the right direction. One result might be the gradual decrease of violence on network television."

Meanwhile, the woodcutter can begin by altering his own life, by teaching his children the gentle violence of love, and by supporting those movies and television programs that mirror the positive side of each of us as well as reducing his own consumption of violent ones that he now finds hard to resist. While he is certain that the pornography of violence is clearly more dangerous than any pornography of sex, the evidence is not clear and compelling to everyone. So to try to force his point of view on every one who disagrees with him would be an act of violence itself.

The woodcutter and his wife can and will direct the viewing habits of their children as best they can. After all, there are many good alternatives on television, and if the woodcutter would only remember to send that $15 check to his public television station, there might be even more.

And there are books and records and concerts and zoos, and, best of all, just sitting around the house and talking to each other for a change. There are many good things we all can do.

The traditional answer to any frontier phenomenon, of course, is censorship. But is not censorship, without a clear and compelling danger, a clear and compelling danger itself?

INTERMISSION

"If any word or expression is of such a nature that the first impression it excites is an impression of obscenity, that word ought not to be spoken nor written or printed; and, if printed, it ought to be erased."

—THOMAS BOWDLER

"Sticks and stones can break my bones, but words can never hurt me."

—CHILDREN'S SAYING

"An adult needs pornography as a child needs fairy tales."

—HENRI POINCARÉ

"Behind the initiation to sensual pleasure, there loom narcotics."

—POPE PAUL VI

"What's it all about?"

—ALFIE

REEL FOUR

Censorship and the Movies

> *No one knows what is good*
> *Who knows not what is evil*
> *And no one knows what is true*
> *Who knows not what is false.*
> —EDGAR LEE MASTERS,
> *Spoon River Anthology*

On the eve of my twelfth birthday, under the sign of Leo the Lion, and up on the roof of my uncle's garage, Roman Cracow showed me a pornographic picture.

I'll never forget it.

Though I can't remember what it was.

I think it was a homemade job, a sort of Molotov magazine that Cracow created himself by tracing the bodily outline of Sheena the Jungle Girl or Wonder Woman or Little Lulu (I can't remember which) together with Bomba the Jungle Boy or Captain Marvel or The Little King (I can't remember which), and filling in the details with a purple crayon. Cracow was the Marquis de Sade of our block, and though he scrambled my brain for years to come, I know there was a Cracow by another name in his past too, just as I am sure there is one in yours as well. Sexual maturity comes on the day we can look back on our Cracows with humor and forgiveness.

Naturally, however, it wasn't long until I saw my first forbidden movie. A foreign job. Branded "morally objectionable in part for all" by the Legion of Decency, the voice of movie morality for Catholics like me. The Legion was an excellent guide for finding out what was bad.

The Catholic bishops of America established the Legion in 1934 to stir church members to keep away from movies that stir the senses. Priests urged parishioners to see only those movies the Legion sanctioned and to boycott those the Legion condemned. Once a year at Sunday Mass, we stood up after the Gospel, raised our right hands, and recited the Legion oath. It was a grave affair, almost as sacred as the Pledge of Allegiance, and anyone who didn't repeat the words was considered at best a troublemaker and at worst a moral leper.

The Legion classified movies into five categories, essentially not bad, almost bad, bad, worse, and worst. The worst, or "condemned," movies like *The Pawnbroker, The Children of Paradise, Martin Luther,* and *Jules and Jim* were lumped together with movies like *Mud Honey, Faster Pussycat, The Bare Kitten,* and *The Dirty Girls.* The not bad, or "morally unobjectionable in part for all," movies like *Henry V* joined forces with *Godzilla Meets the Monsters* to advance culture and morality in the United States.

Without the classification, I would not have been able to discriminate in choosing my first bad film. I didn't want to go all the way out-of-bounds and catch a "condemned." If a Studebaker scrambled my brains on the way home from a "condemned," I would die and go straight to hell. But if it was only a "morally objectionable in part for all," I could talk my way into staying in purgatory. Since I knew purgatory was a foregone conclusion anyway, I decided to stick just one foot over the frontier and see a partially immoral movie.

So, at thirteen years old, I rode my black Schwinn up Clark Street, chained it to a lamppost in front of the Vogue theater, and laid down my 35 cents to see a unique mixed combo. Though I'm really not sure, I think the lead movie was *Serpent of the Nile,* starring Rhonda Fleming and rated "almost bad." The bottom half of the bill was a foreign film, rated "worse," or "morally objectionable in part for all," called *La Strada.*

While I really can't recall the name of the first movie, just as I can't put together Cracow's concupiscent cartoon, I do remember every scene and almost every line from the officially objectionable *La Strada.* Especially the scene in which the gentle Fool holds up a pebble and tells the sad Gelsomina:

"If I knew what this pebble is for, I would be God who knows everything. When you are born. And when you die. This pebble must have a purpose. If it is useless, everything is useless—even the stars. And you also, you with your artichoke head, you have a purpose too."

The next day I knew I wanted to be a priest and make sad people happy, just like the Fool in *La Strada.* But I didn't dare tell my parish priest that I got the idea from a bad movie. And though I didn't know it at the time, thanks to Roman Cracow and the Legion of Decency, I discovered the difference between obscenity and art at an early age, and, thanks to a morally objectionable movie called *La Strada,* I first began to realize that Roman Cracow has just as much of a purpose on earth as Federico Fellini.

It's hard to believe that the Legion of Decency died a decent death only a decade ago, and rose again as the sophisticated National Catholic Office for Motion Pictures, no longer a legislator of morality through pressure or guilt. For thirty-two years, the Legion scrambled more brains and smeared more works of art than all the Cracows from the beginning of time. But sexual maturity comes on the day you can look back on those days, too, with humor and forgiveness but hope that they don't return in different clothes to haunt someone else.

Today the "new" Legion has new standards, and many Catholic as well as public high schools now show *La Strada* to students in gaily decorated gyms. And sitting in that audience is Roman Cracow, no longer in a crew cut and box toe shoes but doing what he always does and always will do, in a new set of clothes. Perhaps *La Strada* will help unscramble his brain. Perhaps it can't.

Movies mirror reality, and Roman Cracow was born centuries before Thomas Edison photographed a sneeze. Pornography exists not because Roman Cracows grow up and become Russ Meyers but because they belong to our human race. I later learned that one reason *La Strada* was objectionable was that it tended "to arouse undue sympathy for immoral characters." Does that mean that we should reserve our sympathy only for moral characters? So be it. What is sad about censors is that they try so hard to break the mirror but never look at the face in the mirror and say, "Hey, that's me." They don't seem to realize that even Roman Cracow has a purpose and that they, in their own way, are Roman Cracows too.

The Supreme Court's 1973 decision that local communities should act as little legions of decency has fortunately had little impact so far. Like the Supreme Court itself, they can't seem to decide what is or is not obscene. The result is confusion, a mild sort of apathy, and a growing feeling among the police that they have more important things to do than judge dirty movies. But the possibility always remains, from Albany, Georgia, to Anchorage, Alaska, that decent citizens will use existing laws to legislate morality for everyone else.

It's a practice as old as time. The Hebrew farmer who allegedly put together the book Genesis in 900 B.C. included legislation for eating apples. And we all know how Adam and Eve reacted to forbidden fruit.

"Whatever one's attitude to sex is," writes Otto Rank, "it cannot be denied that a great part of its attraction arises from curiosity, from its being kept secret and forbidden."

If it wasn't first forbidden, *I Am Curious (Yellow)* would have been in and out of the Evergreen theater in less than a week. Censorship often has the reverse effect of making certain movies more desirable than they really are and sometimes more arousing than they would be if never repressed at all. As Theodore Reik says, "Repression surrounds the desired objects with an allure they do not have otherwise, and attributes to them power and peril beyond reality." Censorship not only permits and fosters but also tends to glamorize and glorify preoccupation with sex. And the same would hold true if we tried to censor violence. As we saw in Reel Two, the censor is often the pornographer's best friend. Fortunately, works of art like *La Strada* always survive the smears, but while they are being repressed, both the art and the audience are officially condemned as degrading or degraded, debasing or debased, dehumanizing or dehumanized. By creating obscenity, censorship itself is obscene.

The word "censor" comes not from the Hebrew, however, but from the Latin *censere,* meaning "to evaluate," "to tax," or "to take away." Or all three. In ancient Rome, the censor was a magistrate who assessed the community, levied taxes, and regulated its morals and manners. If Jesus of Nazareth had not rendered unto Caesar what was due unto Caesar, the censor would have marked a *nota censoria* next to his name. And a centurion would have taken him away the very next day.

Censorship comes in many forms and so is as difficult to discuss as pornography itself. Psychologically, we all censor ourselves by building a wall between our ego and our id. Individually, we censor *Deep Throat* by going to see *The Longest Yard* instead, or vice versa. As parents, we censor *The Mod Squad* by turning on *The Waltons*. Last year, members of a Nazarene church in Battle Creek, Michigan, found a private way to combat what they felt was sinful television programming. They burned their own television sets. Few people would argue with any of the above methods.

Public censorship, however, refers to the official repression of any kind of expression considered dangerous to any established order. A government censors information by stamping "classified" on documents that the public may or may not have a right to see. A teacher censors books by taking away *The Catcher in the Rye* and assigning a book report on *Huckleberry Finn*. A church censors movies by creating the Legion of Decency. A police officer censors both books and movies by confiscating those that are considered unacceptable to society at large. Last year a Philadelphia divinity student wrote a religious book that was a best seller in Pennsylvania's Amish country. But for the wrong reasons, according to author Dan Neidermyer. Members of the Amish faith did not like the book's point of view, raised $4,000 to buy out the first printing, burned them all, and persuaded the publisher to print no more. Many people would argue with some or all of the above methods.

The purpose of any censorship is protection—of values, standards, order. And few people argue against the goals. But the method of public censorship is to take something away from everyone—through pressure, guilt, or force. And many people argue with that. The basic thing censorship takes away, they say, is choice. And choice is the essence of freedom. So censorship ultimately takes away freedom.

Neither censorship nor freedom, however, is like pregnancy. One can never be just a little bit pregnant, but, as Richard Kuh points out, "one *can* be just a little bit censored," and freedom "need *not* be wholly unconfined." Unfortunately, it doesn't always work out that way.

For example, two centuries before Christ, a Chinese emperor named Tsin Chi Hwangti built a great wall to protect his people from a clear and present danger called an army. We could call that censorship with freedom. Then he built a bonfire and burned all literature to protect his people from frivolity. We do call that censorship without freedom. And that's what it usually looks like.

Forty-eight years before Christ, a Roman ruler named Julius Caesar sacked Alexandria and burned all the historical documents in its library, at that time the most important record of civilization in the world. After the birth of Christ, both Christian and Arab crusaders kept going back to that library, and throughout the centuries they destroyed more than seven hundred thousand priceless manuscripts. A Moslem soldier named Omar went so far as to heat his bath water with these flaming ideas: "These books are either in accordance with the teaching of the Koran or they are opposed to it. If in accord, then they are useless, since the Koran itself is sufficient, and if in opposition, they are pernicious and must be destroyed." Today everyone would argue against that. But not everyone did then.

In 1524, a Belgian king named Charles V made a list of books he thought were heretical, and twenty years later the church released its Index of Forbidden Books. Both lists censored books with religious viewpoints considered dangerous at the time. The list of writers censored as religiously dangerous throughout the centuries include Confucius, Galileo, Martin Luther, John Calvin, Charles Darwin, Pierre Teilhard de Chardin, Ivan Illich, Hans Küng, and Matthew,

Mark, Luke, and John, to name a few. Even today, if you check that list, you'll see that not everyone everywhere would argue against it, in principle if not in practice.

In 1791, a new country called the United States of America added the Bill of Rights to its Constitution. The First Amendment reads: "Congress shall make no law respecting an establishment of religion, or prohibiting the free exercise thereof; or abridging the freedom of speech or the press."

But in 1813, President Thomas Jefferson learned that citizens would not always feel that way. He ordered a philosophy book from his local bookstore. A shallow critique of Isaac Newton, the book was probably beneath Jefferson's intelligence, and he simply slipped it away on a shelf. But a policeman who picked up another copy at the bookstore found it blasphemous and dangerous. He arrested the bookstore owner. A horrified Jefferson cleared the man and wrote him a letter:

"Is this then our freedom of religion?" he asked. "And are we to have a censor whose imprimatur shall say what books may be sold and what we may buy? And who is thus to dogmatize religious opinion for our citizens? Whose foot is to be the measure to which ours are all to be cut or stretched? Is a priest to be our inquisitor? Or shall a layman, simple as ourselves, set up his reason as the rule for what we are to read and what we must believe? It is an insult to our citizens to question whether they are rational beings or not; and blasphemy against religion to suppose it cannot stand a test of truth or reason. Let us hear both sides if we wish."

Censorship too, then, is a frontier phenomenon, prohibiting specific material considered objectionable by a specific part of a specific culture at a specific time. But who is to judge what is out-of-bounds for everyone and what is not? A president? A policeman? A minority? A majority? Everyone? Or each one? History shows that what a few judged objectionable yesterday many honor today, and what many honor today may be judged objectionable by others tomorrow. Censorship is objectionable because, unlike the rain, it not only sullies what it seeks to make clean, but it never falls equally on the just and on the unjust, and is therefore unjust itself.

In 1948, the United Nations signed a Universal Declaration of the Rights of Man:

"Everyone has the right to freedom of opinion and expression; this right includes freedom to hold opinions without interference and to seek, receive, and impart information and ideas through *any media* and *regardless of frontiers.*"

Obscenity didn't become a frontier phenomenon until the eighteenth century, not for any lack of obscenity but because there weren't many books around until that time. But in 1725, a British judge put both facts together and ruled that it was a common law crime to publish an obscene book. He did not define obscene. But the King's attorney general did argue that Edmund Curll's *Venus in the Cloister,* or *A Nun in her Smock,* "tends to corrupt the morals of the King's subjects and is against the peace of the King." Private morality became synonymous with public law. "Destroying that is destroying the peace of the government, for government is no more than publick order which is morality. My Lord Chief Justice Hale used to say, Christianity is part of the law and why not morality too?" Today, many people would find *Venus in the Cloister* less immoral than *Jack and the Beanstalk,* but many didn't then. That decision paved the way for all the obscenity censorship to come.

In 1815, a Philadelphia court bluntly accused Jesse Sharpless, an art dealer, of showing "a certain lewd, wicked, scandalous, infamous, and obscene painting representing a man in an obscene, impudent, and indecent posture with a woman, to the manifest corruption and subversion of the youth, and other citizens against the peace and dignity of the commonwealth." The judges did not look at the picture themselves for fear of inflicting permanent damage on their "eyes or ears."

Six years later, Boston police arrested two booksellers for selling the debutante of all obscenity cases, *Fanny Hill.* Again, the judges refused to look at the book; they knew, by golly, what was obscene without looking at it. Ironically, a hundred and fifty years later, another Massachusetts court turned down their *Fanny* again by 4 to 3 while ruling in favor of *Tropic of Cancer* 4 to 3, whereas at the same time a New York court declared *Fanny* the winner over *Tropic* in a reverse 4 to 3 decision. So much for consistency.

In 1857, England passed a salvo of laws against obscenity without saying what constituted obscenity. It took ten years until the Lord Chief Justice came up with an opinion that would influence courts on both sides of the Atlantic for a century. Sir Alexander Cockburn thought "the test of obscenity is this, whether the tendency of the matter charged as obscenity is to deprave and corrupt those whose minds are open to such immoral influences, and into whose hands a publication may fall."

A century later, United States Justice Jerome Frank would take that opinion a step farther and ask if the matter charged as obscenity, apart from any social or artistic merit, constitutes a "clear and present danger" to society as well as to individuals. And in 1956 he would point out that there is no clear evidence that it does and that there is some clear evidence that it does not.

Meanwhile, back in the 1870's, after the most brutal war in our nation's history, a dashing young bluenose named Anthony Comstock knew that the evidence was in. In 1873, he started the New York Society for the Suppression of Vice to attack the "hydra-headed monster of obscenity." The Society lobbied Congress into passing a law against sending "obscene or crime-inciting matter through the mails." Known as the Comstock Law, it forbade "every obscene, lewd, lascivious, or filthy book, pamphlet, picture, paper, letter, writing, print, or other publication of an indecent character" and any article, medicine, or prescription that might "prevent conception" or "produce abortion." The penalty was "not more than $5,000 or imprisonment not more than five years, or both, for the first offense." Most grateful, perhaps, were mailmen who were relieved of a heavy burden.

Within two years, Comstock's army had seized, in one way or another, "130,000 pounds of bound books" as well as "60,300 articles made of rubber for immoral purposes"—a collection of pornography that might turn Al Goldstein, the editor of *Screw,* blue with envy. But included in the poundage were the works of Rabelais, Zola, Balzac, Daudet, and Thomas Hardy. Near death in 1915, Comstock boasted that he had "convicted persons enough to fill a passenger train of 61 coaches, 60 coaches containing 60 passengers each, and the 61st almost full, and destroyed over 160 tons of obscene literature."

Comstock's death in 1915 only gave birth to new vice societies in states and cities from coast to coast. And these societies had a wider target than ever before—the movies.

Movies, in fact, had been censored prior to exhibition in theaters by local boards since 1907. But in 1915, perhaps encouraged by Comstock's departure from the scenario, an Ohio distributor brought the Supreme Court into the plot. Is not precensorship illegal? he wanted to know. We don't pre-censor books or magazines. Are not motion pictures, too, protected by the free press and free speech guarantees of the Constitution?

No, said the highest court, they are not. "The exhibition of moving pictures is a business, pure and simple, originated and conducted for profit, like other spectacles, not to be regarded as part of the press of the country or as organs of public opinion."

Within five years, however, movies became more than a business. They became a way of life. As a war that nobody wanted came to an end, the screen turned silver and laborers and housewives worshiped a galaxy of stars—sex symbols like Rudolph Valentino and Theda Bara, Douglas Fairbanks and Mary Pickford. A new morality, mirrored in movies like *Foolish Wives* and *Blind Husbands,* fascinated millions of Americans. It also outraged millions more, those who lived in what was then called "Gopher Prairie"—a geographical expression for a state of mind, found both east and west of the Hudson, which we now call Middle America.

It's hard to believe, but parents suddenly found a generation gap between themselves and their children. Young people danced, drank, smoked, and did God knows what else in the rumble seats of Packards. "It's done!" a daughter tells her parents in *This Side of Paradise.* "You can't run everything the way you did in the nineties!"

Women won the right to vote, but, believe it or not, demanded more. "Solitary dishwashing isn't enough to satisfy me, or many other women," complains the heroine of *Main Street.* "We're going to wash 'em by machinery, and come out and play with you men in the offices and clubs and politics you've cleverly kept for yourselves." Some women went so far as to burn their corsets.

Most men didn't mind. They were more excited over the battle between Dempsey and Carpentier, the fight of the century, billed as the first and last million-dollar match in history.

In 1921—over fifty years before Dick and Liz, Vanessa

and her baby, and the tragic deaths of Sharon Tate and Bruce Lee—scandals rocked Hollywood like a series of earthquakes. Police collared funnyman Fatty Arbuckle after an all-night party and accused him of the death of a pretty young girl. On a chilly night in February, a visitor found director William Desmond Taylor sprawled on the rug of his apartment with a bullet in his chest. Producer William Ince died of "acute indigestion" aboard William Randolph Hearst's luxurious yacht. Marion Davies and Charlie Chaplin were accused of a secret love affair. Wallace Reid, rugged star of *The Deerslayer*, died of an overdose of drugs. Sensational tabloids like the New York *Daily News* painted Hollywood as an opium den. And the citizens of Gopher Prairie knew that the movies were turning America into Babylon.

Some even blamed movies for the crime that was sweeping the country, exemplified in the notorious Leopold and Loeb case but not exemplified in the Sacco and Vanzetti trial that dragged on from 1920 until 1927.

Hollywood needed a savior fast. The moguls asked President Harding for his top deliverer, Postmaster General William Hays. Hays preferred to serve his country, but after considering an offer he couldn't refuse—$100,000 a year—came to Babylon West to deliver it from evil.

For a while, Hays had things under control and the studios went to the bank with profits from films like *The Phantom of the Opera, Robin Hood, Ben Hur,* and *The Mark of Zorro.* But when sound came to the movies in 1926, movies became more than a business, more than a spectacle, and more than a way of life—they began to mirror society in ways more vivid and compelling than newspapers or magazines ever could. It wasn't long until the sons and daughters of Anthony Comstock hit the ceiling. And soon every state in the union had a censorship board.

So in 1930, Hays put teeth into his production code, and

soon drew up the guidelines we saw in Reel Three. A review board previewed the films, and those that met the guidelines received a seal of approval. As we saw in Reel Two, sex was split into twin beds until the early '60s, and, as we saw in Reel Three, violence kept on changing its clothes.

Morally speaking, all was quiet on the Western front until Clark Gable told Vivien Leigh in 1939 that frankly he didn't give a damn. But Clark was King. So the public didn't give a damn either.

In 1940, Howard Hughes, the Clifford Irving of his time, hoaxed Hollywood by ballyhooing a movie he hadn't even begun. He started to promote *The Outlaw* with ads that asked, "What are the two greatest reasons for Jane Russell's rise to stardom?" And he designed a special brassiere to hold the heavy reasons. Twenty-five years later, Ralph Ginsberg would go to jail for mailing a magazine called *Eros* from Blue Ball, Pennsylvania, and we all know what happened to Cliff. Hughes merely suffered the indignity of not receiving a Code Seal. But he opened his movie anyway in 1946, and, because of censorship through pressure groups, a minor movie was turned into a major hit.

Darryl F. Zanuck didn't have Hughes's chutzpah and took *Forever Amber* away from Philadelphia forever because Catholics in the City of Brotherly Love threatened to boycott all 20th Century Fox films. In that movie, Linda Darnell, formerly the Blessed Mother in *The Song of Bernadette,* tries to seduce Cornel Wilde, though he never would have known it if he hadn't read the book.

Meanwhile, throughout the '30s and '40s, independent producers not bound by the Code made a series of "clap operas"—movies about the dangers of promiscuity, venereal disease, and other spin-offs—and sold them to grind houses also not bound by the Code. Somber films, they were careful to make a moral point in black and white in order to avoid trouble, and set the pattern of escape for the Technicolor nudies of the '50s. In *Child Bride,* a backwoods teen-ager wants to get married. Her voluptuous schoolteacher tells her it is wrong, and for her sound advice she is stripped to the waist, is tied to a tree, and receives a sound whipping. The lithesome teen-ager jumps into an old swimming hole for a long shot skinny dip, but as she rises from the deep she sees the error of her ways. The audience gets both a glimpse of flesh and a moralistic slap in the face at the same time. Other clap operas included *Honky Tonk Girl, Hopped Up,* and *The Wages of Sin.* The wages of sin were high for the distributors, a group of men who called themselves the Forty Thieves and proved for the first time that censorship can be skirted.

An interesting exception to the clap-opera rule was the notoriously successful *Mom and Dad,* which simply showed the birth of a baby. Made in the '30s, it kept popping up in theaters for the next two decades. It skirted the censors by bringing along a nurse or a doctor to answer questions after the movie was over and by having two separate showings, one for women in the afternoon and one for men at night. When I was about twelve, I remember a photograph in the Chicago *Tribune* showing long lines of people stretched around the block of the Rialto Burlesque Theater to see *Mom and Dad.* Real moms and dads wouldn't talk about the movie. The ads for the movie were sensational and everything about it seemed lurid. I would have liked to have seen it but I was afraid. Twenty years later, I was glad to hold my wife's hand as she gave birth to our first son, Christopher, and to do the same as Jeffrey was born two years later. What was lurid in 1951 had become beautiful, albeit messy, in 1971.

It is surprising that a baby was born at all on the screen of the Rialto back in the '50s. At that time, Chicago had a police-controlled censorship board that previewed films before they were allowed to appear. The director of the board felt that "children should be allowed to see any movie that plays in Chicago. If a picture is objectionable for a child, it is objectionable period."

Other boards had other standards. Memphis censors took away *Brewster's Millions* because Jack Benny's buddy, Rochester, is "too familiar," then they went on to segregate *Curley* from movie houses because white and black school-children play together on the same screen. Atlanta censors judged *Lost Boundaries* out-of-bounds because a black doctor and his wife pass for white. New York censors found *Damaged Lives,* a movie about venereal disease sponsored by the American Social Hygiene Society, damaging. And Maryland censors banned a documentary about Poland that was made in Poland because it "fails to present a true picture of Poland."

A modest movie called *The Miracle* passed a pre-censorship test in New York and opened at an art house around the feast of the Immaculate Conception. An Italian movie, it features Anna Magnani as a simple-minded peasant who gets seduced by a stranger because she believes he is St. Joseph. She has the baby because she believes he will be the Messiah. The New York Commissioner of Licenses believed the movie was "officially and personally blasphemous," and saw to it that it was aborted before Christmas. The importer Joseph Burstyn opened the new year by taking the commissioner to court. The movie returned before St. Valentine's Day.

The Legion of Decency condemned it. Cardinal Spellman equated it with "the greatest enemy of civilization, aetheistic Communism." The New York Board of Regents' censorship committee took away Burstyn's license. Burstyn took the regents all the way to the Supreme Court.

In 1952, the Court ruled that "a state may not ban a film

on the basis of a censor's conclusion that it is sacrilegious." Justice Stanley Reed indicated that movies, like newspapers, radio, and magazines, *are* guaranteed freedom by the First Amendment. A state can license movies, but the Supreme Court must "examine the facts of the refusal in each case to determine whether the principles of the First Amendment have been honored." As with books, the Supreme Court was now the final arbiter in disputes over specific motion pictures.

Miraculously, it still took five years for *The Miracle* to play in Chicago after a local censor refused to give it a license. In 1961, a film distributor refused to give his movie *Don Juan* to the Chicago board. His point was not the possible obscenity of his film but the possibility that precensorship itself is obscene and unconstitutional. The Supreme Court, in a split 5 to 4 decision, seemed to contradict their 1952 decision and ruled that movies are not "necessarily subject to the precise rules governing any other particular method of expression." Precensorship of motion pictures is not unconstitutional.

It's curious that when *I Am Curious (Yellow)* was being precensored, you could buy a paperback of the script together with photographed highlights in bookstores, drugstores, and airports. We're no longer afraid of books, but movies continue to threaten us. Perhaps they frighten us because their magic takes place in darkness. Nobody bragged about throwing up after *reading The Exorcist.* And, oddly enough, *The Exorcist* was never exorcised by the censors.

As we saw in Reel Two, censors are mainly concerned about sex. And the archetypal attitude is perhaps best summed up in the following instructions a censor gave to his staff: "In the scene in which the girl is tortured while hanging by her hands, eliminate all views of her with her breasts exposed." Lenny Bruce got into trouble by telling us that we can't bear to look at bare breasts unless they're mutilated.

One local court, reviewing a nudist magazine during the time of the nudies, offers a detailed description of obscenity that may tell us more about censors than about obscenity:

"The woman has large elephantine breasts that hang from her shoulders to her waist. They are exceedingly large. The thighs are very obese. She is standing in the snow in galoshes. But the part which is offensive, obscene, filthy, and indecent, is the pubic areas shown. The hair extends outward virtually to the hip bone."

It all depends on your point of view. I would have judged that the galoshes were obscene.

Kurt Vonnegut's fictional Senator Rosewater gives a definition of obscenity that seems to encapsule them all:

"Obscenity is any picture or phonograph record or any written matter calling attention to reproductive organs, bodily discharge, or bodily hair. . . . The difference between pornography and art is bodily hair."

In 1957, the Supreme Court cemented the ambiguous relationship between sex and obscenity by saying on the one hand that they "are not synonymous," and in the next breath declaring material obscene "which deals with sex in a manner appealing to purient interest . . . that is, material having a tendency to excite lustful thoughts." The snake swallowed its tail.

In 1957, of course, the difference between pornography and art *was* bodily hair, just as it was a navel in 1894. And from 1957 to 1966, there would be a total of 55 separate opinions among justices on what is or is not obscene.

Perhaps censorship is obscene because it stands in the snow in galoshes.

Dorothy Sayers once observed that "a man may be greedy and selfish; spiteful, cruel, jealous and unjust; violent and brutal; grasping, unscrupulous and a liar; stubborn and arrogant; stupid, morose and dead to every noble instinct—and still we are ready to say that he is not an immoral man."

Movies that portray any or all of the above have seldom been in danger of the censor's scissors either, but those that depersonalize, or even personalize, sex are. If we can accept a pornography of piety, of propaganda, and of violence, why can't we accept a pornography of sex? Of course, we could turn the argument around and decide to supress all distortions of reality, all mirages, all movies that might be potentially dangerous—and the result would be little left to see. Who can find unanimous agreement on what is dangerous and what is not?

We can't even agree on what is or is not obscene.

I'm not alone in finding television commercials obscene. And I'm not so much offended by Debbie, who exploits my sexuality to stimulate me to fly her and National to Florida, as I am by Ed Reimer, who cups my house in his hands and exploits my insecurity to stimulate me to buy All-State home insurance. I know some people who find the homespun homilies of *Mister Rogers* more distasteful than the flying fists of *Mannix*. Perhaps we should take a lesson from Oscar the Grouch on Sesame Street, who shows us that one person's trash is another person's snack. "The social and human risk of censorship," writes Michelson, "turns out to be far greater than the risk in allowing one another our moral eccentricities. And so, because denying our freedom to choose trash would violate our human dignity and thereby undermine the commonweal, I conclude that censorship is indeed bad."

If you walked past the New World Theater on West 49th Street on March 1, 1973, you saw black letters pinned to the marquee: JUDGE CUTS THROAT. WORLD MOURNS. If you watched the news on WNBC that night, you saw film critic Gene Shalit tug on his walrus mustache and say that while he personally felt that *Deep Throat* was trash, "I care more about individual liberty than about one rotten movie. . . . We do not want to err, but if err we must, let us err on the side of freedom."

I have tried to present one woodcutter's point of view that public censorship is unworkable, unjust, dangerous, and obscene. "From a religious point of view," writes Richard Hettlinger, "the objection to obscenity laws is that they deny the principle of responsible adult judgment. We cannot educate people to moral maturity by excluding from the public scene whatever we regard as debased and inadequate. In a mature society, obscene literature would not be suppressed but ignored."

"Censorship," concludes Kyle Haselden in *Morality and the Mass Media,* "is hostile to authentic morality wherever it limits man's freedom, wherever it narrows the range of his individual decision and personal choice, wherever it restricts his access to any knowledge and any ideas."

The best censorship is not to take something away from everyone, but to maintain an atmosphere that provides everyone with alternatives and to support those that are positive. "The point of education," writes Lawrence Rubinoff, "is not to force men to virtue solely as a means of avoiding punishment; it is rather to persuade men to virtue by rewarding the performance of virtuous acts."

"In the long run of history," says Whitney Griswold, former president of Yale, "the censor and the inquisitor have always lost. The only sure weapon against bad ideas is better ideas."

"Do not be overcome by evil," Paul warns, "but overcome evil with good."

If we don't like the reflections of obscenity, either those

cast in blue or those dipped in blood, the solution is not to break the mirror but to face up to the face in front of the mirror. From my point of view, censorship begins and ends on the spot where we're standing.

REEL FIVE

The Last Frontier

"I am marked like a road map from head to toe with my repressions. You can travel the length and breadth of my body over superhighways of shame and inhibitions and fears."

—ALEXANDER PORTNOY

Clouds came over Chicago, and shadows spread across the roof of my uncle's garage. A cool breeze moved in from the lake, blowing westward away from home. A gentle voice called softly from a faraway porch, "Michael, your supper's ready."

"That's my mom," I said. "I gotta go."

Another voice bellowed from a nearby basement, "Cracow, come and get it!"

"That's my old man," Roman said. "I gotta come and get it. Listen now, you don't tell nobody about them pictures. You understand?"

I shook my head yes.

"Okay. You're cool. Go ahead."

I climbed carefully over the edge of the roof and shimmied down the raingutter, thinking I should have slid through it instead. Roman hung to the edge of the rail and jumped. He didn't even hurt his feet. Then he grinned, gave me a wink, and waved good-by.

I wandered down the alley in a daze. I bumped into a garbage can, tripped over a mattress, and mumbled to myself in front of a coalman. Later when my mother looked me in the eye, I knew that she knew that I knew. But I didn't think she knew that I knew that she knew. So I kept my mouth shut.

A few weeks later, I discovered the mystery of my own body, and the discovery was as frightening as it was surprising. It happened by accident at the end of a *Flash Gordon* chapter on the *Saturday Morning Playhouse,* sponsored by Red Goose Shoes. The Hawk Man, saliva dripping down his chin, his wings flapping excitedly, cornered a flimsily clad Dale Arden. Dale breathed heavily, her two reasons for stardom puffing up and over her halter. Hawk Man stretched out a hairy hand. Unconsciously, my hand moved too. Dale clutched her flesh. The Hawk Man leered. Dale screamed. And the planet Mongo exploded in a pair of Wrangler jeans. "Tune in next week!"

I couldn't wait a week to shed my guilt. That afternoon, I raced my Schwinn down Addison Street toward St. Andrew's Church. Confessions began at 4 P.M. I sought out a ninety-year-old priest from Sicily who had hair in his ears. I entered his box. The shutter slid open. He groaned. I confessed my shame, and prayed he wouldn't probe. Thank God, he was pastoral. He asked me if I took cold baths. I said no. He said take. He asked me if I slept with the window open. I said in the summer. He said winter, spring, and fall. He asked me if I ran around the block. I said only when somebody was chasing me. He said run.

Absolved, I crept out of the box, said ten Hail Marys, and pedaled home. That night I took a cold bath. Then I ran around the block. At night I slept with the window open. The next morning I woke up with a terrible cold. I had to stay in bed all day, daydreamed about Sandra Dee, and did the same bad thing again.

During Advent, we had an eighth-grade retreat. The priest who gave it carried a huge cross in his sash like a sawed-off shotgun. He spoke of the dangers of the solitary sin. He did not tell us it would make us go crazy. Cracow told me that. And proved it. But the priest did tell us it was a mortal sin. And scared the hell out of us. Then he gave us each a book called *The Rocky Road to Maturity,* which would help us build strong souls by teaching us how to build healthy bodies.

I took the book home. I studied the pictures of strong men with bulging biceps doing exercises on dining room tables, on rooftops, and in front of three-way mirrors. Do the exercises and I could have veins in my arms too. The author, a retired Army chaplain, talked about the evils of smoking and drinking and masturbating. "But don't worry," he said, "if you can't break the grip of this pernicious, health-destroying, life-sapping habit—self-pollution—all at once. It may take weeks, months, even years. Why, I once knew a young man who was poisoned by the serpent of self-abuse for twenty years! But he met me, took my Rocky Road to Maturity, and became Mr. Universe in one short year!" Well, since I had only been poisoned twice, and since I intended to do the exercises anyway, I figured one more slip couldn't hurt me much.

The next Saturday I raced my Schwinn down Addison Street for afternoon confessions. For the first time, I learned that semen is sacred and that the natural use of one's genitals is procreation, or to make babies. What I had done was against the laws of both God and nature. Now I really felt bad. I always thought the natural purpose was to go to the toilet. I was a pervert. I felt so guilty in my cold bath that night that I did it again. And then felt even worse. I wanted to drown myself. But then I remembered hell.

The next Saturday I raced my Schwinn down Addison

Street for afternoon confessions at St. Andrews. More shame. More guilt. Leading to more sin. Leading to more shame. Leading to *ad nauseam.*

Four years, two Schwinns, and several Sicilian priests later, I was cured. But I'm afraid that neither the priest with a shotgun cross nor the chaplain's *Rocky Road to Maturity* had anything to do with the cure, though they may have had a lot to do with the disease. The real change may have been due to a growing interest in books or basketball or movies or Linda Rodríguez, or all four. Probably I just grew up.

Adolescence for anyone, of course, is something to get over with as soon as possible, and while I've humorized some of my highlights (to cover up embarrassment as well as to entertain), I haven't distorted the reality of what it was like in the '50s and no doubt all the decades before it. But I don't blame the religious educators of my past for teaching a shameful view of sexuality that surely caused many of the problems they were trying to solve. After all, how were *they* taught? Sexual maturity begins on the day we can admit to our superhighways of shame and cheerfully accept not only ourselves as we are but also all those who traveled with us to the spot where we now stand. It is from there, perhaps, that we take our first step on the rocky road to full maturity.

One thing seems clear though: a false sense of religious guilt tends to prolong an adolescent preoccupation with sex. Modesty is healthy, but shame is immature. "Shame," writes Andrew Greeley, "works against laughter, joy, merriment, singing, dancing, painting, creating, frolicking. It is so obvious that it is these things shame destroys that we have had to create religious systems . . . to persuade us that spontaneity, joy, merriment, love-making are evil, and that shame is a good thing because it is keeping us from evil. Shame really triumphed with the influence of Jansenism and Puritanism."

And its influence remains. "If, in today's sex films," writes Amos Vogel, "the 'pornographic' element predominates, this is because they are produced within the context of a sexually repressed society. The huge financial success of hard-core films cannot be explained in any other manner." But, as we saw in Reel Two, it is largely people my age and older who grew up in a culture that regarded sex as shameful who are sending the producers to the bank.

Station yourself in front of a skin-flick show. You won't see many, if any, people in their early twenties buying tickets. And I can't help suspecting that because their generation has grown up in a religious culture that is learning to accept sex as joyful, not shameful, that many of them have less need to prolong an adolescent fascination with sex.

In any event, during the past decade, religious attitudes toward sex have changed dramatically. Religion too is a frontier phenomenon, constantly reinterpreting old traditions in light of new revelations. Religion, writes Teilhard de Chardin, "does not leave things behind, but, as it rises, it leans on them for support, and carries along with it the chosen part in things." We are on the road to choosing a healthier view of sexuality that may someday eliminate the superhighways of shame.

And, when that happens, many of today's hard-core films will be looked upon as nothing more and nothing less than amusing anachronisms. "Our frequent censorial agitation," muses Vogel, "our titillating scandals, and cautious see-sawing regarding 'it' will undoubtedly be a source of much merriment to future generations."

And evolving religious attitudes, based on "the chosen part in things," will have much to do with this change.

In the Bible, the overall attitude toward sexuality, including nonprocreative sex, is accepting and positive. It soars highest in the superlative Song of Songs, with graphic descriptions of playful, sensual sex that have come to be interpreted by the church as an appropriate symbol for spiritual union with God. Even Paul, who was cautious about the subject since he felt the second coming was near and there were more important things to do, was positive about sexuality and compared the union between a man and a woman to the relationship between Christ and his people.

But Christianity, until recently, has selected little of the Bible's positive point of view toward sex. Instead of carrying along the "chosen part in things," our churches seem to have taken their cue from a father of the church who long ago spoke darkly about "the disease of lust" that infects us all. It's not nice to beat a dead horse, especially a thoroughbred, but as historian Derrick Bailey points out, "St. Augustine must bear no small measure of responsibility for the insinuation into our culture of the idea, still widely current, that Christianity regards sexuality as something peculiarly tainted with evil."

In fairness to Augustine, it should be stressed that one can never isolate a theology from the culture in which it was developed. Augustine was a Manichaean (the body is evil) before becoming a Christian. His thinking was influenced by the stoical culture he lived in, a culture that held that pleasure for its own sake was shameful.

Clement of Alexandria was simply being Alexandrian, not Christian, when he told every woman "to blush at the thought that she is a woman." Origen was so carried away by contemporary attitudes toward sex that he cut off his testicles to avoid wet dreams. It worked. The great Thomas Aquinas was reflecting a cultural emphasis on celibacy when he said that every man who "loves his wife too ardently is an adulterer." Luther, of course, felt marriage was superior to virginity, but he too was a child of his time and, because of the "brutelike quality of passion," considered sex a necessary evil. John Calvin, also a brilliant theologian and reformer, tried to protect his flock from "the licentiousness of the flesh, which unless it be rigidly restrained, transgresses every frontier." These views spread to Great Britain, and the pilgrims carried them over on the Mayflower to America where we've been running with them ever since.

Even Jewish Americans became Puritan Americans by trying to melt in the puritan pot. The early Hebrews of history, writes G. Rattray Taylor, "believed strongly that one should enjoy the pleasures of life, including those of sex, and some teachers held that (on one's) last day one would have to account to God for every pleasure that one has failed to enjoy." Jewish novelist Herman Wouk writes that "what in other cultures has been a deed of shame . . . has been in Judaism one of the main things God wants men to do. If it also turns out to be the keenest pleasure in life, that is no surprise to a people eternally sure God is good." Portnoy has a complaint not because he is Jewish but because he is American.

Like Augustine, Calvin, and Portnoy, our attitudes toward sex have been shaped not so much by Scripture but by the culture we were raised in. And now, in the midst of a cultural revolution, we may be judging some of its manifestations as obscene not because they have to do with sex, but because for a long time we have considered sex itself obscene.

But we are also beginning to consider again "the chosen part in things." Andrew Greeley, an Irish-American celibate priest, distinguishes between the Demon of Shame and the Angel of Eroticism and stands on the side of the Angel. "The Erotic Angel tells us that it is all right to be charming, that it is virtuous to be seductive, that it is reasonable to be spontaneous, and that it is sensible to let our playful, dancing, singing, hand-clapping imp out of the bottle. The imp may not be the whole of your personality, but he is an important part; to hide him is both false to yourself and to the God who created yourself." By his life-style, Greeley is also one of many modern celibates who prove that sexuality and celibacy are not mutually exclusive. A person who freely chooses celibacy as a life-style remains a sexual person. Sexuality is a rich reality that extends far beyond its genital aspect.

The American Lutheran Church (Missouri Synod) officially recognizes the goodness of sexuality by stating strongly that there is "no room for a false asceticism in the Christian view of sex. Sex is not 'evil' or 'dirty.' . . . Prudery has failed miserably. It made matters of sex secretive and unwholesome for the child, lustful for youth, and then often resorted to face-saving moralisms." During the past decade, most Protestant churches have released similar points of view.

A tiny news item in the New York *Daily News* tells of an Episcopal priest in Denver who tells his parishioners that they would be a lot healthier if they viewed sex not as something distasteful but as a gourmet meal. "In the sexual area," says the Rev. Marion Hammond, "all of us begin at a disadvantage because we've all been taught lousy things about sex —the body is evil, sex is sin, fantasy is ugly." Hammond and his wife, Opal, run a five-week sex education course for adults. "Good sex is like gourmet dining," the rector says. "It's not the main course—the entree—but the surroundings, the appetizers, the relationship with the other person."

If that sounds like Masters and Johnson coming to church, the real Masters and Johnson do write in *Redbook* that "mutual pleasure sets a seal on emotional commitment," and they suggest that the best sex takes place in the context of fidelity, or, in another word, marriage. Spice may turn out to be the plural of spouse. In any event, fidelity, with or without a certificate, is one of the "chosen parts" of religious tradition, and it is now being freely reaffirmed in our more liberated culture.

It's interesting that as religious culture is beginning to appreciate contemporary values, contemporary culture is beginning to appreciate religious values. "As for the new morality," writes William Emerson, "it includes a heightened and broadened appreciation of sex and more sexual activity of the heterosexual variety for the married and unmarried in every age group. But a great part of this takes place within the context of love, devotion, and a monogamous intent, inside or outside of marriage."

Max Lerner, in a column called "The Return of Marriage," points out that "we are living in an era of freer marriage forms," but he observes also that "if marriage is rooted somewhere in basic human needs, then the greater sexual freedom may spell the conditions under which good pair-bonds will survive and prevail."

"What is the latest word from the sexual frontier?" asks *Time* magazine. "It may be 'retreat.'" Anthropologist Gilbert Bartell, who coauthored *Group Sex,* now finds "a retreat from sexual frivolity." Feminist Ellen Frankfort, author of *Vaginal Politics,* feels "no doubt that all the experimentation and kinkiness are declining. Now there's a strong desire for connectedness." "Swinging," observes *Penthouse* editor Jim Goode, "has died a natural death."

It will no doubt rise again, but cultural trends and religious attitudes tend to be moving in the direction of both tolerance and responsibility toward sexual behavior. "The movement of American society toward reducing sex to animal-like conduct is about to end," predicts sociologist Amitai Etzioni, and the pendulum is swinging back "to a new synthesis, a new middle." Biologist Robert Kolodny finds that the "strictly mechanical, hedonistic approach to sex, while espoused by some, is relatively rapidly falling to the wayside."

And these changes can also be glimpsed both in movies and in the people who pay for them. Not only are some adult filmmakers trying to graft flesh to human hearts and minds, but many adult filmgoers are beginning to abandon the hardest hard-core shows. To try to draw them back, several adult theaters that used to show a single hard-core film for $5 now show three or more at a bargain basement price. The Orleans theater in Manhattan advertises a "New Policy! Adult Film Bonanza! New Triple XXX Rated Show! $1.99 at ALL times!" Up the block, the Tivoli offers a "7 Hour Marathon" for only three bucks. "Just like in Scandinavia after pornography became legal," says Al Goldstein, "the people of the United States just aren't supporting the industry like they used to." And censorship, since there is now so little of it, has nothing to do with the change.

Perhaps a growing maturity does.

As religion and culture grow closer together, what is needed, as always, is the healthy balance of freedom and responsibility that sociologist Etzioni feels is about to come. To help it happen, Presbyterian minister David H. C. Read suggests a modern approach to ethics that is neither moralistic nor hedonistic. The mature person chooses to plant his or her feet in "the dynamic middle," described as a religious stance that expresses both a loyalty to tradition and a sensitivity to the new needs and learnings of our age.

An Illinois housewife, reacting to an article against pornography in *Marriage* magazine, puts it this way: "True, I would not want my ten-year-old son exposed to filthy magazines in our neighborhood. But I fear, more than that, a return to the repression of sexuality which I knew as a Catholic child. Our bodies were 'bad' and 'dirty' and the Sisters told us not to wear patent leather shoes because our petticoats would be reflected in them. Surely, this type of mentality is just as damaging to a child as any porno shop. I ask that we seek a happy medium, in which sexuality is neither vulgar nor forbidden."

Today many parents view their sexuality in positive ways and transmit this attitude to their children. What they really want to know (my wife and I do anyway) is the best way to pass on moral values to their children in a rapidly changing world. At the moment, I'm all in favor of sexual freedom as long as no one gets hurt. But when my children reach age eighteen I know I'll feel differently. How do I guide them? I also know that masturbation should be neither discouraged nor encouraged. But how do I convey to my sons whatever it is that's in between? Theoretically, I have all the answers. Practically, all I have are questions.

Many schools, public and parochial, now teach ethics through such courses as Character Education, Moral Development, and Public Values; and sex education, of course, is gradually becoming a reality in both primary and secondary schools. It is essential, I think, to include parents in the same learning processes, not only to help them educate their own children but to help them grow themselves. A shared road to maturity may be more difficult to pave than the old path of repression, but it is far less likely to crumble and much more likely to achieve its goals.

In any event, our attitudes toward sex will never be the same as they were in the '50s. They will continue to evolve both cyclically and spirally. But there is ample evidence to believe that they are growing healthier, not worse. And perhaps we should be grateful that many external boundaries have been erased. That leaves only one frontier left for us to cross—the last frontier—*the one within.* And that's the most exciting one of all.

As we've seen, even movies, like *Last Tango in Paris*, are moving in that direction now. And as *we* grow within, other films will grow with us, exploring more than exploiting but, we hope, always entertaining. We simply have to allow some movies to mirror sexuality through a glass darkly in order to allow others to show us who we are and what we might become. And someday, if we begin to focus more on ourselves than on our shadows, we may even become the sexually mature and religiously open society we'd like to think we already are—and cross that last frontier, the one within.

As a matter of fact, I wouldn't be surprised if many of us live to see it happen.

But pornography also includes violence, and there is more than one religious understanding of violence in Scripture and tradition too. The Bible both condemns and defends it, in both the Old and the New Testaments. So anyone with a good I.Q., a decent vocabulary, and armed with a Bible can make a case for or against it to fit any situation—as many have throughout history.

For two centuries, Christian crusaders engaged in violent battles with Moslems to take back the land where the Prince of Peace was born. Both Christians and Moslems could prove that God was on their side. Later the church developed theological principles for a "just war," but the principles, of course, could be applied only through one's point of view. So a few years ago, Terence Cardinal Cooke told American soldiers in Vietnam, "You are friends of Christ by the fact that you come here," while Pope Paul VI deplored the war publically and never tried to justify it. Theologically, a war is just or unjust when you say it is or it isn't. And that depends on what side you're on.

Also, as Charlie Chaplin says in *Monsieur Verdoux*, "numbers sanctify." So Hiroshima is good, My Lai is bad, and the man of despair who kills his family and fires the last bullet into his skull is doomed for sure. Should it not be just the opposite? Or are they all the same? "Just as all of life is made out of the same flesh," writes William Emerson, "all of violence destroys life. And all of violence is a piece. Violence against other races, against other men's children, against women, against strangers and friends, violence against the earth itself—all of it is a seamless garment. It covers our lack of reverence for all living things."

One thing is certain. And that is change. During the '70s, our religious attitude toward violence may be changing almost as rapidly as our religious attitude toward sex in the '60s. I am far from alone in being shaken by the possibility that a violent world leads to brutal movies whose cumulative effect could condition us to casually accept that world as it is. And I find it interesting that this increasing concern over violence comes hot on the heels of an increased appreciation of sex. Psychologists suggest a connection between the repression of sex and the expression of violence, and our affirmation of sexuality may have much to do with what seems to be a growing desire to negate violence, reflected repeatedly in movies and on television.

— Obscenity is taking on a whole new meaning, and many religious thinkers now agree with Herbert Marcuse that "obscene is not the picture of a naked woman who exposes her pubic hair, but that of a fully clad general who exposes his medals rewarded in a war of aggression; obscene is not the ritual of the Hippies but the declaration of a high dignitary of the Church that war is necessary for peace."

Unfortunately, there are few major Christian writers who, like the French theologian Jacques Ellul, have explored the obscenity of violence in depth, though I can think of many who have written at length about sex. I can't blame them. Sex is easier. But the times are changing. And there are more important things to talk about.

Slowly, we are beginning to realize that the violence we do to others, subtly or crudely, we do to ourselves. And we are growing disturbed by the reflection of ourselves in the mirror. It's not even a single looking glass but a fun house of mirrors that assault us from every angle, forcing us to accept the image and challenging us to change the reality. "If a man accepts a certain image of himself," writes Rubinoff, "he will often behave according to it, then mistakenly accept this behavior as evidence of the truth of his self-image. It is, in other words, entirely possible that one's image of oneself, whether or not it is well founded, may become a 'self-fulfilling prophecy.' " The movies are reflecting what we ourselves believe ourselves to be and, in fact, often are. But just as sexuality is only a part of our nature, so is our samurai instinct only a piece of the whole. The images on the screen will begin to brighten only when we begin to bring out the best in ourselves.

"We have to begin," writes R. D. Laing, "by admitting and even accepting our violence, rather than blindly destroying ourselves with it, and therewith we have to reason that we are as deeply afraid to live and to love as we are to die." In fact, we have always found it easier to be overcome by violence than to overcome violence with love. But if religion teaches us anything at all, it is that "the chosen part" is love. And that love is stronger than death.

"It is not brute force we need," writes Teilhard de Chardin, "but love, and therefore, as a start, the recognition of a Transcendent which makes universal love possible."

All religions teach that physical violence—the violence of hate—can be transcended only by spiritual violence—the violence of love. A love that doesn't take but gives. A love that doesn't care if it seems to lose. A love that desires neither medals nor thank-yous. A love that applies to individuals, communities, and nations. "Choosing different means," writes Ellul, "seeking another kind of victory, renouncing the marks of victory—this is the only possible way of breaking the chain of violence, of rupturing the circle of fear and hate." We've known this since Eden, but only recently, perhaps, have we begun to believe it.

Now as then, our choice is between love and hate, hope and despair, faith and fear. And our growing distress over the glorified images of hate on the screen may be an important step toward making love a vivid reality in our everyday world. We may never re-create Eden, but we can, by re-creating ourselves, begin to plant kindness on the piece of earth each of us stands on each day. And again I wouldn't be surprised if many of us live to see signposts to Eden—the last frontier—before we die. After all, sex is tricky, but love is something we can teach our children without ever saying a word. And both we and our children make up tomorrow.

Finally, a balanced view of pornography has to reckon with the fact of change, for, existentially, pornography is nothing but change. As we have seen, new values and vocabularies, roles and life-styles, as mirrored in movies and on television, are forcing us to ask with *Alfie,* "What's it all about?"

We are living at a higher rate of unpredictability than ever before in the history of humanity. And while some of us thrive on change, others try to censor it, and few of us try to understand it. But all of us, no matter what our point of view, are suffering the polarizing effects of rapid change. A few years ago, Alvin Toffler argued in *Future Shock* that humanity cannot be swept beyond established frontiers without suffering disturbance and disorientation. Today even the frontiers have been swept away.

The future came yesterday, and many of us are unprepared to deal with it.

Some of us, in fact, would like to go backward.

And why not? Life used to be a lot simpler. Or so we think.

Permanence—of ideas and values, mores and standards—used to be normal. Today the norm is transience. And transience turns everything upside down. Yesterday's fad is today's nostalgia and today's craze turns to melancholy before it fades away.

Many of us even wonder what our religion is all about now. Our grandparents never worried about that. They felt close to God. Or so we think.

But how do we feel?

Do we feel close to God? Or does God seem far away? Has he gotten lost in the turmoil of our times? How can we recapture the sense of his presence in our changing world?

One way to begin is to accept the fact that there is no going backward. Our modern world evolved in less than ten thousand years, but in the last two hundred years it has changed faster than in all the previous millennia. In the last two decades it has changed faster than in the previous two centuries. And the rate of change continues to accelerate like a carousel out of control. While we might be wise to control the pace of change, we'd be foolish to try to abolish it. Evolution, in movies and in life, is as natural as birth and death. To try to censor it is to bite our own tongues.

"No matter what reactions we may have to current events," writes Teilhard de Chardin, "we ought first to reaffirm a robust faith in the destiny of man. Even if that faith is already there, it must be fortified."

What will humanity be like at the end of this century?

Despite my optimistic point of view, I really have no idea, but neither does anyone else. So no matter what happens next, I prefer to have faith in our common destiny and would rather look forward with hope to an unknown future than look back over my shoulder at a past that can never return. I don't even know what our attitudes toward sex and violence will be a decade from now, but I do know what they were like a decade ago, and despite detours and potholes, I believe we've already come a long way toward a new maturity.

"Instead of dreading what lies ahead," asks Helen Colton, "why not welcome it as a new and exciting adventure, with much pain but also with much promise? It is the obligation we owe to this experience called Life to make our futures different from our pasts."

And yet, no matter what we choose to do, tomorrow will simply not be the same as today, and we can't even begin to make it better until we first accept that fact. Psychoanalyst Erik Erikson is one of many who point out that "in our society at present, the 'natural course of events' is precisely that the rate of change should continue to accelerate up to the as-yet-unreached limits of human and institutional adaptability." Alvin Toffler warns, "During the next thirty or forty years, we must anticipate not a single wave of change, but a series of terrible heaves and shudders."

The Roman Catholic Church, for instance, has seen more changes in the decade since Vatican II than in the previous century. And it's not an exaggeration to expect even deeper changes in all Christian communions in the next twenty years than all those made since Paul left Tarsus twenty centuries ago. We are already living in a world where the surreal has become the real—a world of urban communes and empty seminaries, teen-age gurus and tentmaker priests who speak in tongues and eat eucharistic pizzas. And perhaps our religious leaders must be among the first to recognize the inevitability of change in life more than in film and to reaffirm a hope in a God who is neither static nor still but who makes all things possible and all things new. It may be an initial step toward reconciling those who like to ride on the crest of change with those who seek the safety of the harbor.

It is certainly in harmony with the Holy Spirit. Episcopal bishop John E. Hines points out that "in a world of sometimes agonizing change, the Church cannot be less than the 'radical minister of change.' God willing, it should be more than that. But it cannot be less, and still be faithful to a God whose spirit continues to make all things new."

Two thousand years ago there was no room at an inn for a woodcutter from Nazareth and his pregnant wife, Mary. Today there should be room in our churches and temples for everyone, and for every point of view. That is the lesson of Bethlehem. And who knows what a woodcutter and his wife might give birth to? Perhaps a samurai. But maybe a nobleman. You never can tell. Fresh epiphanies await the church as long as its door is open.

A similar step toward sanity is for each of us, as individuals, to undergo the most radical change of all—*metanoia*—a change of heart that not only tolerates but tries to understand different points of view. We are all members of a common humanity caught up in an era of change that may mark a turning point in human history. "We have reached a crossroads in human evolution," says Teilhard de Chardin, "where the only road which leads forward is towards a common passion." Only through reconciliation can we begin to act intelligently and together, neither blindly rejecting nor blindly accepting change, but directing it for the good of us all.

"This time, like all times," wrote Ralph Waldo Emerson a century ago, "is a very good one, if we but knew what to do with it. Old deeds for old people and new deeds for new."

It's going to be a bumpy road to maturity for the rest of the century—no doubt about it—but I don't want to miss a jolt as all of us hopefully stumble together toward Bethlehem, the new Eden, the last frontier—the one within. The century to come could be the beginning of a wonderful surprise. Not the second coming of the Son of Man on a cloud of fire. But a sudden awareness that he has never left us at all.

Change, violence, and sex—these three are inescapable elements of pornography. I look at them not as a theologian but as a woodcutter with a personal point of view. But I wouldn't be surprised if someday a genuine theologian, perhaps a German schooled in Heidegger and Kant, puts everything together and writes a theology of pornography—a definitive book (good for five years). Meanwhile, all we can do is appreciate the past, enjoy the present, and look forward to the future. And if things get too rocky, well . . . we can always go to the movies.

TRAILERS

Film critic Robert Warshow once observed that "a man watches a movie and the critic must acknowledge that he is that man." If Warshow were alive today, he would no doubt use the word "person," but from his point of view, *any* critic, male or female, should try to reflect "the actual, immediate experience of seeing and responding to the movies as most of us see and respond to them." And, for better or for worse, that's the point of view I've taken with me behind the blue door.

But there are other points of view. And other books on movies, pornography, censorship, religion, violence, and sex. In an effort to make this book a fairly fast read from beginning to end, I've put all notes and comments, with occasional bibliographical suggestions, in the following trailers.

Books on or related to the subject of this book could fill a library, so I'm highlighting only those which have had some influence on the development of my own point of view, even though many of them represent viewpoints far to the left or to the right of mine—depending on your point of view on where mine is located.

In any event, every point of view is important, and each is valid, and the books cited below are not only valuable in themselves but can lead you to even others if you wish to explore certain aspects of the subject in further detail. Perhaps it is only by studying all points of view that we can come to a mature viewpoint that is uniquely our own.

—The quotation from James Agee on the epigraph page comes from his first movie column for *The Nation,* Dec. 26, 1942. That quote, and others referred to in this book, can also be found in *Agee on Film, Vol. I: Essays and Reviews by James Agee,* published by Grosset & Dunlap in 1972. Poet W. H. Auden wrote in 1944 that Agee's movie column "is the most remarkable regular event in American journalism today. What he says is of such profound interest, expressed with such extraordinary wit and felicity, and so transcends its ostensible—to me, rather unimportant—subject that his articles belong in that very select class—the music critiques of Berlioz and Shaw are the only other members I know— of newspaper work which has permanent literary value." To read Agee's reviews, three decades after he first wrote them, is to heartily agree with the poet.

PREVIEW

—Richard Hettlinger's *Sex Isn't That Simple,* published by The Seabury Press in 1974, is a mature evaluation of the evolution of sexual values among today's youth. Written primarily for college students, the book is perhaps equally valuable to parents struggling to understand "the new morality" on campus.

—The example of the film critic comes from Helen Colton's *Sex After the Sexual Revolution,* published by Association Press in 1972. I am grateful to Ms. Colton not only for the reference but for providing me with a perspective on the sexual revolution that I find as pertinent today as when she first put it to paper.

REEL ONE—*A Definition of Pornography*

—Richard Randall's *Censorship and the Movies,* published by the University of Wisconsin Press in 1970, is an authoritative work that fleshes out theory with fact.

—Mr. Valenti was speaking to a California audience on behalf of the MPAA in 1969. I found the quote in *Censorship in America* by Olga G. and Edwin P. Hoyt, published by The Seabury Press in 1970. A so-called juvenile book, *Censorship in America,* like many books addressed to young people, presents an interesting overview of the subject that can inform and entertain older persons too.

—Kenneth Turan and Stephen F. Zito, writing in *Sinema: American Pornographic Films and the People Who Make Them,* quote Dr. Schneider who describes obscenity as "sexual material which lies just on the other side of the currently accepted boundary line, regardless of the specific content, (that) has by virtue of its location the power to excite." *Sinema,* published by Praeger in 1974, is not only the most comprehensive survey of the pornographic industry but also features interesting interviews with such insiders as Russ Meyer, Marilyn Chambers, Gerard Damiano, Harry Reems, and others.

—Although most of the movies discussed in this and the following reels come directly from memory, I am indebted to at least four indispensable reference books for supplying specific dates, facts, and other information: (1) Leslie Halliwell's *The Filmgoer's Companion,* Avon Books, 1970; (2) Georges Sadoul's *Dictionary of Films,* University of California Press, 1972; (3) Stephen H. Scheuer's *The Movie Book,* Ridge Press and Playboy Press, 1974; (4) *Sinema,* referred to above.

REEL TWO—*Sex in the Movies*

—Ira H. Carmen's *Movies, Censorship and the Law,* published by the University of Michigan Press in 1966, remains a classic despite the rapid changes that followed its publication.

—The German artist was architect August Endell, quoted by Frank Whitford in *Expressionism,* Hamlyn, 1970.

—Roger Ebert's article "Sex and Violence in the Movies," in the March–April 1972 issue of *The Critic,* published by The Thomas More Association in Chicago, is witty and wise and says a great deal about the subject in a very few words. Perhaps because he is not a New Yorker, Ebert may not be one of the more widely known, but is surely one of the most astute film critics writing today. Incidentally, he also wrote the screenplay to Russ Meyer's *Beyond the Valley of the Dolls.*

—Richard N. Smith's *Getting Into Deep Throat,* a Berkley paperback published in 1973, is an amusing and well-written account of the film, from its initial conception to its final censorship in New York. Most amusing are actual transcripts of the court trial in which the movie was declared obscene.

—The quote from Richard Kuh comes from his essay in *Censorship and Freedom of Expression,* edited by Harry M. Clor for Rand-McNally in 1971. He is also the author of *Foolish Figleaves? Pornography in and out of Court,* published by Macmillan in 1967.

—John Drakeford's definition is from his *Pornography: The Sexual Mirage,* with cartoons by Jack Hamm, and published by Thomas Nelson in 1973. "By its very nature," says Drakeford, "a mirage lives in the individual's mind. In the case of a weary traveler, his thirst fosters the image of an oasis with springs of water, verdant pasture, palm trees, and the promise of everything the traveler needs. But it has no reality. As fast as the traveler approaches, just that fast his mirage retreats from him. This is exactly the nature of pornography. It is fiction removed from fact." As fiction often is, I thought. In any event, while Drakeford's book is a little too conservative for my comfort, I must also confess that many of his arguments against arguing *for* pornography moderated some of my own original attitudes.

—Drs. Eberhard and Phyllis Kronhausen's *Pornography and the Law* is a 1964 Ballantine Book that almost every other book on the subject written after 1964 refers to in one way or another, pro or con.

—Peter Michelson's *The Aesthetics of Pornography,* published by The Seabury Press in 1971, is recognized by most experts on the subject as a brilliant presentation that goes beyond the conventional rationales of pornography on the grounds of its redeeming social value, and argues for its legitimacy as literature, a distinct genre that can provide insight into the darker side of our nature. "The moral basis of pornographic literature," he argues, "is that it is an imaginative avenue to greater knowledge of human being." While Michelson focuses primarily on literature, his insights are applicable to films as well.

—Charles Rembar's *The End of Obscenity* is a 1968 Bantam Book with much influence on writings that followed. Lawyer Rembar successfully defended the book *Fanny Hill* before the U.S. Supreme Court in 1966.

—The Episcopal Church study appears in Urban Holmes's *The Sexual Person,* published by The Seabury Press in 1970. "The result of seven years of reading, reflection, conversation, writing and testing on the part of a number of concerned adult churchmen," it presents a careful but positive view of sex in light of both religion and culture.

—Howard Moody's article "Toward a New Definition of Obscenity" appeared in the Jan. 25, 1965 issue of *Christianity and Crisis,* Washington, D.C.

—The quote from SIECUS comes from a statement to the Commission on Obscenity and Pornography in April 1970. The complete *Report of the Commission on Obscenity and Pornography* was published by Bantam Books in 1970, and while it is indispensable, it is difficult to find. The Government Printing Office, at this writing, has limited copies available, and unless you write directly to the commercial publisher you may not be able to get a copy unless you have a good used-book store nearby.

REEL THREE—*Violence in the Movies*

Many interesting books on war movies exist, some lavishly illustrated, but for a brief but comprehensive overview, with photos, you might wish to look into *The War Film* by Norman Kagan, one in a series of books on movie history and movie stars published by Pyramid Publications. The Kagan book also contains a bibliography of other books and articles on the topic. You might also enjoy Pyramid Publication's *James Cagney* by Andrew Bergman and can look forward to Jimmy's own autobiography at about the same time this book appears in print.

—Arthur Schlesinger's *Violence: America in the Sixties* appeared as a Signet Broadside Book, published by the New American Library in 1968.

—Pauline Kael's review of *Clockwork Orange* appeared in the Jan. 1, 1972, issue of *The New Yorker,* and can also be found in the 1974 Bantam paperback, *Deeper Into Movies,* a collection of Ms. Kael's reviews that won her a National Book Award. Little, Brown & Co. published the cloth edition in 1973.

—The reports from the National Commission on Violence, the Surgeon General's Advisory Committee on Television and Social Behavior, and hearings before the Subcommittee on Communications of the Committee on Commerce of the United States Senate are all available from the U.S. Government Printing Office, Washington, D.C.

—Konrad Lorenz's views on aggression come from an interview in the Nov. 1974 issue of *Psychology Today* with Richard Evans.

—Leonard Berkowitz's study appeared in an article entitled "Impulse, Aggression and the Gun," published in the Feb. 1964 issue of *Psychology Today.*

—Lawrence Alloway's *Violent America: The Movies 1946–1964* was published by The Museum of Modern Art, New York, in 1970, and is an important contribution not only to film criticism but to a fuller understanding of our society and culture.

—Both quotes from Thomas Shine appear in the March 21–24, 1972, records of the hearings before the Senate Subcommittee on Communications, available from the U.S. Government Printing Office.

—While I believe that most parents are aware of the power of television upon their children, and have the common sense to guide them, two new books on the subject have just come out in 1975 and concerned parents may wish to consult them. They are: (1) *The Family Guide to Children's Television: What to Watch, What to Miss, What to Change and How to Do It,* by Evelyn Kaye, Pantheon Books; and (2) *Go Watch TV! What and How Much Should Children Really Watch?* by Nat Rutstein, Sheed & Ward.

Intermission

—An anticensorship chrestomathy appears in Eli M. Oboler's *The Fear of the Word: Censorship and Sex,* published by Scarecrow Press in 1974. But the book is much more than a collection of quotes. Oboler's synthesis of censorship throughout the ages as it relates to the word, and his analysis of the implications, make it a basic book on the subject.

Reel Four—*Censorship and the Movies*

—Roman Cracow's *real* name has been changed to protect the guilty. But, like Holden Caulfield found out, now I sort of miss him. "Don't ever tell anybody anything. If you do, you start missing everybody."

—Richard Kuh's concept of "Censorship *with* Freedom of Expression," found in Clor, *Censorship and Freedom of Expression,* concerns mainly the protection of children, and I would not argue with him on that score at all. In *Foolish Figleaves?* he proposes legislation or statutes that would protect minors while allowing freedom for adults.

—I owe some of the examples in this chapter to those referred to in Hoyt, *Censorship in America,* mentioned previously.

—If you wish to learn more about Anthony Comstock, check out your local library for *Anthony Comstock, Roundsman of the Lord,* by Heywood Broun and Margaret Leech, published by Albert and Charles Boni in 1927, although you will find examples of Comstock's work and influence in most books on the subject of censorship.

—*Hollywood in the Twenties,* by David Robinson, a 1970 Warner Paperback Library book is not only a complete survey of movies from 1920 to 1930 but a brief and interesting look at the culture in which they were made. It is part of an international film guide series that also has books on movies of the '30s and '40s.

—The example of the girl being tortured comes from Richard Randall's book, cited above, as does the one about the girl in galoshes. Senator Rosewater's definition comes from Kurt Vonnegut's *God Bless You, Mr. Rosewater,* a Dell paperback first published in hard cover by Holt, Rinehart & Winston in 1965. Both books, each in its own way, are funny and wise.

—*The Other Six Deadly Sins,* by Dorothy Sayers, was published in London by Methuen in 1943.

—Richard Hettlinger's religious point of view on censorship can be found in Clor, cited above. For an interesting debate on "Should There Be Censorship of Pornography?" read the article in *Sexual Behavior,* Dec. 1971, between Hettlinger and conservative Harry M. Clor. And for a strong argument by a conservative *against* censorship, read David Burdnov's "Obscenity" in the July 1974 issue of *Playgirl.*

—Kyle Haselden's *Morality and the Mass Media,* published by Broadman Press in 1968, is a valuable study with a personal point of view.

—Lawrence Rubinoff's profound book, *The Pornography of Power,* published by Quadrangle in 1968 is more about philosophy than pornography, but the points he makes, whether you agree with them or not, are indelible. "My underlying assumption," he writes, "essentially a metaphysical one, is that every human act or phenomenon is an expression of the whole nature of man and proceeds, therefore, from the primordial character of man's being-in-the-world." Michelson operates from a similar assumption in *The Aesthetics of Pornography,* and though both books are written for different purposes, together they make up a scholarly approach to art and life that complement each other in many ways.

—Other books on censorship, in addition to those cited in Reel Two, that you might find helpful are Harry M. Clor's *Obscenity and Public Morality: Censorship in a Liberal Society,* University of Chicago Press, 1969, and Morris L. Ernst and Alan U. Schwartz, *Censorship: The Search for the Obscene,* published by Macmillan in 1964. In any event, one book or article on this subject, once you're into it, invariably leads you to another. And every book related to the subject of pornography treats the topic of censorship in one way or another.

REEL FIVE—*The Last Frontier*

—Andrew Greeley distinguishes between the Demon of Shame and the Angel of Eroticism, among other devils and angels within our nature, in *The Devil You Say,* published by Doubleday in 1974. He also gives his personal point of view on the subject in *Sexual Intimacy,* first published by The Thomas More Association in 1973 and published as a paperback by The Seabury Press in 1975.

—The quotes in this Reel from Teilhard de Chardin come from two sources: (1) *Building the Earth,* published by Dimension Books in 1965, and (2) *The Divine Milieu,* published by Harper & Brothers in 1960. Both, particularly the latter, are excellent introductions to Teilhard's religious optimism. And Harper & Row has several other Teilhard classics, such as *The Future of Man, The Phenomenon of Man,* and *Hymn of the Universe* which, from my point of view, are inspiring, informative, and totally illuminating. If you wish to reaffirm your own faith in the destiny of humanity, you must read Teilhard de Chardin.

—Amos Vogel's *Film as a Subversive Art,* published by Random House in 1974, is, from my point of view, a landmark book on cinema, even though it's fairly recent. His subject is the evolution, in movies as in life, from taboo to freedom. And I know that I'll want to read it over many times. The book has vivid illustrations of subversive images in cinema, and the author's writing ability is superb.

—Derrick Bailey's *Sexual Relation in Christian Thought,* published by Harper & Brothers in 1959, is a standard book on the sexual attitudes of the Christian church throughout history.

—I found the Taylor quote on the early Hebrews in *The Playboy Philosophy,* a booklet published in 1963 by the HMH Publishing Company. Herman Wouk's philosophy can be found in *This Is My God,* published by Dell in 1964.

—For a definitive study of celibacy as a life-style not only with religious but with countercultural value, you might be interested in Donald Goergen's *The Sexual Celibate,* published by The Seabury Press in 1975.

—The statement of the Lutheran Church appears in *Sex and the Church,* ed. by Oscar E. Feucht for Concordia in 1961.

—Masters and Johnson's *Redbook* article appeared in the Jan. 1975 issue, and the book *The Pleasure Bond,* upon which they based their article, was published shortly thereafter by Little, Brown & Company.

—William A. Emerson's brisk book, *Sin and the New American Conscience,* published by Harper & Row in 1974, speaks wisely not only on the new morality as it pertains to sex and violence but with regard to business and politics as well. His, too, is a hopeful point of view.

—The Lerner column on marriage appeared on January 31, 1975, a few days after scientists Etzioni and Kolodny

were predicting a return to the "middle" at the annual meeting of the American Association for the Advancement of
Science. Interestingly enough, many other scientists agreed
with this point of view. None disagreed.

—The *Time* magazine article appeared in the Nov. 25,
1974, issue.

—David H. C. Read's *Christian Ethics* was published by
J. B. Lippincott in 1969. Perhaps the pioneer book in this
area was Joseph Fletcher's *Situation Ethics,* published by
The Westminster Press in 1966. And perhaps these two
books evolved from two books by Bishop J. A. T. Robinson,
Honest to God, and *Christian Morals Today,* both published
by The Westminster Press in 1963 and 1964, respectively. In
any event, there have been many books written since that
may owe a debt to the above.

—Mrs. Linda Smith of Illinois found her letter to the
editor published in the Dec. 1974 issue of *Marriage* magazine.

—For a fresh look at the just war theory as well as new
insights on violence as it applies to colonialism and racism,
see Robert McAfee Brown's *Religion and Violence,* published by The Westminster Press in 1973.

—Jacques Ellul's *Violence* was published by The Seabury
Press in 1969. An original, Gospel-centered study of this
complex phenomenon, it comforts neither those to the left
nor those to the right of the issue but does offer a forceful
contribution to its further discussion.

—Herbert Marcuse's radical *An Essay on Liberation* was
published by Beacon Press in 1969.

—The quotes from both Emerson and Rubinoff come from
their books cited above.

—R. D. Laing's insights on "Violence and Love" can be
found in the Fall 1966 issue of *Humanitas.*

—Alvin Toffler's *Future Shock* was published by Random

House in 1970. The quote from Erikson comes from that book, too.

—Helen Colton's positive point of view comes from *Sex After the Sexual Revolution,* cited above.

—"That's all, folks!"